It takes a
DOG
to raise a
Village

It takes a
DOG
to raise a
Village

TRUE STORIES OF
REMARKABLE CANINE VAGABONDS

BY RUTH GORDON

WILLOW CREEK PRESS
Minocqua, Wisconsin

Illustrations © 2000 by Peter Ring

Published by Willow Creek Press
P.O. Box 147
Minocqua, Wisconsin 54548

For information on other Willow Creek titles, call 1-800-850-9453.

Library of Congress Cataloging-in-Publication Data
Gordon, Ruth
    It takes a dog to raise a village : true stories of remarkable canine
vagabonds / Ruth Gordon.
        p.   cm.
    ISBN 1-57223-300-1
    1. Dogs--Anecdotes. 2. Human-animal relationships--Anecdotes.
I. Title.

SF426.2 .G67 2000
636.7--dc21   00-026388

Printed in the U.S.A.

Contents

Dedication

This book is dedicated to my husband, Ken,
and to Ben, our first golden retriever. We are grateful
that he was a one-family dog.

Introduction

The idea for this little book all started with Boozer, an incredibly independent dog who spurned confinement and one-family ownership. He lived in the little Minnesota town, Marine-on-St.Croix, where our summer cottage was located. We knew him personally, but our golden retriever puppy became even more intimately acquainted with him, catching his fleas. Boozer first became well known locally. He appeared on local television and was written up in both Twin Cities newspapers. However, after his appearance on *Good Morning America*, he led the life of a national celebrity, filmed by Fuji, and fawned over by reporters and photographers. My first story of Boozer appeared in the April, 1992 issue of *Dog World*. Stories about this vagabond dog's lifestyle continue to intrigue every dog lover who hears about him.

I thought Boozer was one dog in a million, but as I wrote and talked about him, I learned about other dogs who were cared for by a whole community. "It takes a village" has real meaning in many of these dogs' lives. In each instance, there was always a handful of particularly loving persons who shouldered most of the responsibility for the dog's welfare. On a cruise to Alaska, I found the story of Patsy Ann. She lived on the Juneau waterfront and always knew when a ship was arriving long before anyone else did even though she was stone deaf. Fifty years after her death, she was memorialized with a statue of her likeness in a little park at the Juneau docks where the cruise ships arrive. June Dawson, who represents the Friends of Patsy Ann organization in Juneau, Alaska, supplied the information about this independent dog.

Some years later I learned about the *Dog Hero of the Year Award* sponsored by Ken-L Ration dog foods. The 1993 winner, a dog named Weela, took many risks to save other dogs, horses, and people during a two month-long flood in the California town where she lived. While she was not as unorthodox as many of these dogs, her valor during a community crisis certainly qualifies her for inclusion in this book. The author is grateful to Jessie Vicha of McDowell & Piasecki Food Communications, Inc. for providing information about Weela.

Tricksey is the second of these dogs that I knew personally. This golden retriever's community was a nursing home. She brought great joy to many residents for a decade. She tells her story from her own point of view.

The story of *Lampo, The Traveling Dog,* came to my attention through Pennsylvania's Tarmans Books which deals in secondhand and out-of-print animal stories. Elvio Barlettani wrote the book in Italian in the first person. It was translated from the Italian by Alan Houghton Brodrick (Random House, 1963). My recounting of the story of Lampo is based on Brodrick's translation.

Old Drum's story is a little different. His special bond occurred posthumously. When Old Drum, a coon dog, was killed, a whole community took sides in a lawsuit brought by his owner against the alleged killer. The closing appeal to the jury by George Vest, the owner's attorney (and eventual state senator), has been quoted thousands of times. In Warrensburg, Missouri, you can see a statue of Old Drum and a tablet with Vest's words which were spoken 100 years ago. The information about this dog comes from Icie F. Johnson's story, *The Old Drum Story*, and newspaper accounts and pictures graciously supplied by the Trails Regional Library in Warrensburg, Missouri.

Owney, the world traveler, spent his life riding mail trains and ships. He just loved mail bags. Finally, he became the mascot of the United States Railway Mail Service. At his death, he was taken to a taxidermist. Owney can be seen in the National Postal Museum of the Smithsonian Institution. The information about this dog comes from *Owney, Mascot of the Railway Mail Service*, an account of the dog's life compiled by James Bruns and published by the Smithsonian Institution (1992).

My step-daughter, Marion, discovered Red Dog and his statue while visiting Western Australia. Red Dog's story is based on information contained in two small books. The first book, *Red Dog*, by Nancy Gillespie was published in 1983 in Great Britain. The second book, *Red Dog The Pilbara Wanderer*, was written by Beverley Duckett and published in Western Australia in 1993.

Greyfriars Bobby lived over 100 years ago. Tourists who have seen his statue in Edinburgh, Scotland, know that he spent every night on his master's grave for 14 years. After reading Eleanor Atkinson's book entitled *Greyfriars Bobby*, published in 1912, I decided that the story of this spunky little dog's life deserved retelling.

I know of other dogs with atypical lifestyles and most unusual bonds with humans, but the information is often too sketchy for any kind of a story, even a short one. Getting acquainted with these dogs has been a wonderful personal experience. Their loyalty, courage, independence, and illusive inner drives exemplify the canine spirit that so facinates their human observers.

Stories

Boozer

A Town's Dog

Boozer lived by his wit and charm in Marine-on-St. Croix, a town of 606 residents about 35 miles north of St. Paul, Minnesota. Not everyone approved of his personal arrangements— having his own bank account, being his own owner (as verified by his dog license), and being free to roam like no other dog in town. But when he brought national attention to this little town by being on *Good Morning America*, who could argue?

Boozer had his own float in the 4th of July parade, often accompanied by the Booz-ettes marching with bones in their ponytails. He once collected six write-in votes for mayor, rode on the paddle wheeler to celebrate Marine's sesquicentennial, and regularly attended the New Year's Eve dance and the Octoberfest held at the Village Hall. With no owner, you may wonder how this dog managed to maintain this lifestyle for almost fourteen years.

Boozer was mostly basset hound. He had a long muscular body, a beer belly, short legs, and long floppy ears which alternately touched the ground when he waddled along. Bassets do not walk: they waddle. They also look dejected most of the time because their lower eyelids hang down so far, a reminder that the blood-hound is one of the basset's ancestors. Boozer was unable to wag his short tail without wagging his whole body from neck to tail.

Unlike most dogs, Boozer did not wish to please people; he wanted people to please him. His behavior was predicated on that principle, and his life was a testimony to its success. Boozer's other strong characteristics were total self-centeredness and avowed independence. You might say he was a highly successful street person.

The first time I met Boozer, he was lying in the middle of the little road that led to our summer cottage. I stopped the car; he gazed up at me without lifting his head. I honked the horn; he closed his eyes. When I finally drove around him slowly, he kept his eyes closed and concentrated on ignoring me. We quickly learned that Boozer was the new kid on the block. We also were told that he had "strange" ways. Boozer spent much of his time lying in the middle of the road, moving only when he had an errand of his own to do. Everyone— almost everyone—got used to driving around him.

I got used to his ways, but the day Boozer was not in the middle of the road, I knew something was wrong. We learned that someone had run over him. I do not know who did it and never asked, but most town folk suspected that it was one of the someones who did not think he was a cute, eccentric addition to the neighborhood. That was when we discovered that Boozer was nearly indestructable. Less than a week after the accident, Boozer was right back in the middle of the road again. Aspirin and rest had done the job.

Little is known about Boozer's puppyhood because his owners turned him in to the Hennepin County Humane Society when he was about a year old. Once you got to know Boozer, you could easily understand how this happened.

The Humane Society gave the dog to the University of Minnesota Veterinary Hospital. This must have been a tough time for Boozer, as he was used in studies at a research lab. Eventually, the lab decided to give the dog back to the Humane Society for reasons that are not quite clear. However, Ann, one of the lab workers, had come to love Boozer, so she brought him home to her apartment as his new owner.

Something about the apartment displeased him, so he ripped up the sofa cushions the first day he was alone in the apartment. When Ann came home to the mess, she had a serious talk with him. The next day while Ann was at work, Boozer chewed up a very nice down comforter. Ann's distress with his obvious displeasure did not deter her from trying to find him a good home. So, thinking he might like to live in the country, Ann gave him to her brother, Joe, who lived in Marine-on-St. Croix.

Joe was delighted to take Boozer because he wanted a good hunting dog. Joe kept Boozer outside and did not let him in the house. Next door, however, lived the Moffitt family with a little boy and girl, two and four years old. They loved playing with him and they welcomed him into their house when Joe was at work. Boozer loved playing with the Moffitt children. He was so pleased that he stopped going to Joe's house except for food.

Joe tried everything to lure him back but he finally gave up. One day Joe walked over to the Moffitt's house and said, "Here's his leash, dog food, and dish. If this is where he insists on living, *you* take care of him." Because of the children, the Moffitts became his new owners— although *caretakers* is a more accurate description in view of the subsequent events.

When Boozer was not lying in the road, he cruised the entire village. He checked out new residents— human, canine, and feline. He hung around places where he could get a conversation going and, most particularly, he returned to anyone who presented him with food. The St. Croix River flows lazily along the edge of town. Most of the town is situated up several steep hills above the river, so it often took Boozer most of the day to waddle up and down the hills, depending on how many stops he made.

When Boozer cruised, he often picked up other dogs who would cruise with him. Some were stray "no-goods," but some were well-trained dogs who never left their premises except when Boozer came by. Many owners were furious when they found that their animal had literally been lured away from their yards, sometimes for hours of worry and anguish. Such were Boozer's leadership qualities in the dog kingdom. We used to call these cruising canines "the town riffraff." When these packs of dogs approached our house, we got our golden retriever puppy, Ben, into the house as quickly as possible. We were unsuccessful to the extent that Ben caught fleas from repeatedly sniffing this motley entourage.

Several citizens protested Boozer's cruising activities so the city council passed a dog ordinance requiring all canines to be controlled by leash, tether, or fence. It is probably more accurate to say that the Council decided to enforce an already existing ordinance. Boozer was living with the Moffitts when this occurred, so they tied him up in their back yard. What a reaction! Boozer paced and howled for hours on end. A basset's bay is a very persistent howl that humans can tolerate for just so long. With a basset's stubborness, Boozer would not stop his baying except for the few minutes when he took food and water.

He found it unbearable to be thwarted from his usual daily rounds about town. At 10:00 AM, he was used to going to the General Store to meet the bakery truck driver who always had a day-old doughnut for him. Incidentally, this store is "Ralph's pretty good grocery store, where if we don't have it, you don't need it," made famous by Garrison Keillor who lived in Marine-on-St. Croix for several years. After getting his doughnut, Boozer would visit some of the men working in town, locate the old folks with cookies, have clam linguini with the Sormans, arrive at the elementary school just when the bell rang, and find a kid or two who would share an ice cream cone with him.

One can understand why he found it unacceptable to be denied these pleasures. After listening to Boozer's unceasing howling and baying, Claudia Moffitt finally set him free in spite of the leash law. It took him quite a while to forgive her for his ordeal.

Boozer, always on the alert for a better place to hang

out in case things did not go his way, had become acquainted with the new owners of the marina, John and Sandy. In addition to their boat slips and canoe rental business, they had a little restaurant in their main building. On his earlier visits to the marina, Boozer had noticed that business was brisk—with lots of friendly people who were generous about handing out food scraps. Boozer moved in.

Boozer's canine friends were usually permanent residents of Marine-on-St.Croix, dogs who were followers, not leaders, and dogs who had learned not to cut into his territory. Boozer quietly assessed any canine outsider. His dislikes were predicatable. He ignored the meek but took action if he found an outsider intrusive or annoying.

On one occasion during the winter when the river was frozen over, two hunters became more interested in imbibing than hunting. They were almost directly across the river from the marina. They had a young black Lab who became bored and decided to look for action elsewhere. He crossed the frozen river and found Boozer musing on a snow covered dock. The Lab wanted to frolic, but Boozer did not feel playful. Boozer was a serious sort and played very little. This young Lab went beyond play, however. He was a tease. He danced around Boozer, yipping and nipping at his feet.

Boozer finally got fed up, stood, shook the snow off himself, and walked south on the frozen river. Boozer's leadership abilities never failed. The young dog followed him downriver at least a half mile until they were both out of sight. Some hours later, the inebriated hunters came to the marina looking for their dog. By then, no one knew just where either dog was. The hunters returned to inquire about their dog on two later occasions, but by then it seemed ominous. Boozer returned to the marina several days later, but the other dog was never found. Since similar incidents had occurred in the past, John was convinced that Boozer took such animals on well-calculated long and dangerous journeys.

Once, John's suspicion was fairly well confirmed. On a cold snowy night, John drove home through the back-hill road. As he came around a curve, he thought he saw a pile of snow move in the woods. He turned around and drove back to the spot. Suddenly, Boozer came waddling through the snow. Behind him was a mysterious-shaped white apparition. It turned out to be a neighbor's dog, Hoover. The dog was encased in snow and ice and could hardly walk on his ice encrusted feet. Had he not been rescued when John came along, it was unlikely that Hoover would have ever been seen again. While no human will ever know just what happened on those dangerous journeys, it was pretty clear that they were never dangerous for Boozer.

Rick, the dogcatcher (the animal-control officer in the area), arrested Boozer periodically when he could catch him. Some friend always payed Boozer's fine to bail him out of dog jail. While this amused many Marine residents, it infuriated dog owners who were conscientious about controlling their animals. Boozer's detractors could not understand why this town bum could run loose while other dogs couldn't. The big problem, of course, was that Boozer had no owner. No one could control him so no one wanted to take full responsibility for him, but at least three families would have done anything for him — and did.

Boozer even got John and Sandy in trouble with the Health Department one summer. Dogs are not allowed in restaurants. John would explain to the restaurant inspectors that Boozer was not his dog and that he stayed outside, only occasionally sneaking in with a customer. That worked a couple of times, but John finally was fined because the dog always seemed to be there when the inspectors came to check things out. When the inspector decided that the issue of the dog's ownership was irrelevant to the issue of health department regulations, John did his best to let his customers know that the dog *had* to stay outside.

One summer Boozer's fleas were so bad that Sandy had to treat him with flea powder. This displeased him so much that he immediately left his beloved marina and returned to the Moffitts. Just to hedge his bets, he also took up with Todd and Dorothy who lived near the marina with their new baby. After all, the Moffitts might tie him up again!

Some weeks later, Rick caught Boozer again. Claudia

Moffitt bailed him out once more, but this time she decided something creative had to be done. Boozer needed to go to a veterinarian for shots and heartworm pills, he needed a dog license, he had no real owner, and he had no money. Claudia came up with an idea that put him on national television.

First, the idea was to have Boozer take financial responsibility for himself. After all, he was now nine years old. She arranged to have his picture taken for printing on T-shirts. A local photographer took the picture without charge, but not without being insulted by Boozer.

Boozer either liked you or he didn't. Those of us whom he liked were always flattered by his approval, and those whom he disliked always felt a little inferior because of his disapproval. The photo session for the T-shirts elicited one of Boozer's most ungrateful behaviors. Boozer refused to get in the photographer's car so

John had to put him in the car. Thirty minutes later, Boozer was back at the marina. He had jumped out of the car and run away from the photographer.

Finally, Claudia went to the studio with him. The picture turned out very well and the Boozer T-shirts sold out. Both year-round residents and summer people bought them. The proceeds from the sales were placed in a special Boozer checking account at the Marine bank. When someone asked Claudia what would happen if Boozer ran out of money, she replied, "Well, he'll just have to sell more T-shirts."

But that did not solve the owner and license business. Even his best friends did not want to get fined for not leashing a dog they did not own. Nor did anyone want to have the whole town disturbed by his wailing whenever he was tied up. A solution was found. The county agreed that Boozer's license would show that he was his own owner!

With all the major problems under control, Boozer continued his independent vagabond life. He stayed with people who pleased him at the moment, he had multiple sources of food, he continued to drive the dogcatcher crazy, he had his own financial resources, and his town was full of loyal advocates.

Every October the people of Marine celebrate St. Francis day in the town square. The Lutheran minister puts on a Franciscan monk's robe and blesses all the animals that are brought to him. Sometimes a Catholic priest joins him. There are horses, dogs, cats, gerbils, birds, frogs, and whatever living thing a child or adult chooses to have blessed. Each one is blessed individually. Boozer was blessed on eleven St. Francis days. Many residents thought these annual blessings were particularly important for Boozer.

Boozer was written up in all the Twin Cities newspapers and appeared on local television several times.

Strangers in town would come looking for him. When *Good Morning America* did his story, Charles Gibson introduced the segment with, "This is the story of a homeless dog who lives on easy street." They showed his favorite eating spots. They showed his jail, his T-shirts, and his bank statement. His best friends were interviewed while he gave the camera a studied pose. After the show, so many orders came in for T-shirts from all over the country that Boozer never wanted for money again.

After all this, Boozer's celebrity status continued to grow. The town was very proud of his publicity. Fuji films came to Marine to shoot his comings and goings for a full day. Fortunately, this photo session went better than his T-shirt session. According to John, Boozer had never met any Japanese people before and he just seemed to like their looks and the lilt in their voices. There was a big story about him in the travel section of the

London Daily Mail. Other magazines started coming to town to photograph him. There was even a movie offer.

On one occasion, he rolled in something so dreadful that he had to go to a groomer. When it came to the bill, the groomer said, "No charge. It's an honor to take care of such a celebrity." Claudia said, "You know he can afford to pay his own bills," but the groomer would have none of it.

In his later years, Boozer was hit by a car on Highway 95. As he got older, he would rest in the middle of the highway because it was sort of midway between his major destinations. It was nothing like lying in the middle of the little road leading to our cottage! Everyone thought this accident would be the end. But no, the veterinarian once again took care of him successfully. As before, the veterinarian said, "No charge. It's an honor to treat such a celebrity."

Boozer's arthritis started to bother him more and more as he grew older. While he had many friends who watched out for him, the Moffitts and John and Sandy never stopped their special love and care. During his last year, when he could no longer waddle up and down the hills, they drove him. He would spend a few days with the Moffitts; then the Moffits would drive him to the marina. After a few days there, John and Sandy would take him back to the Moffitts where the children gave him great big hugs. In October, 1993, for the last time, Boozer took part in the blessing of the animals on St. Francis day. The pastor spent a little extra time with Boozer that day. Since everyone in town knew that Boozer was old and ailing, it was a special event because his friends had one last opportunity to honor him and be grateful for his life.

Not long after this, Boozer was found to have

untreatable cancer. On a very sad day, he was mercifully "put away" and buried in an unmarked grave in his beloved woods. The next day, all the children in Marine wore their Boozer T-shirts to school. The newspaper report of his death told his story and quoted some of his friends. "He was the one person in town who liked everybody." Well, almost. Boozer had lived long enough to have lost many of his aged friends. One who knew him well helped us all to reconcile his loss. He said, "I am sure he is up there in people heaven going from one of the old ladies who used to feed him to another."

The $350 left in Boozer's bail fund was used for a party to celebrate his life. The marina put up a plaque reading, "Boozer slept here." As one resident said, "Now Boozer is a legend."

Owney

The Globe Trotter

Owney just loved mail bags, whether they were on wagons, mail trains, or steamships. It was a mystery why he was so fond of mail bags but Owney, the Globe Trotter, became the mascot of the United States Railway Mail Service, was preserved by a taxidermist and stands in the Smithsonian National Postal Museum today. There are many unknowns about Owney. No one ever knew where he came from, or how old he was when he was first found lying on top of a mail bag at the Albany, New York, post office. Neither is it clear how he got his name.

His breed is also a mystery. However, his ancestors certainly must have included an Irish terrier regardless of what other breeds were a part of him. He not only looked much like an Irish terrier, but he had some of their traits, such as great courage and a steadfast faithfulness about watching over whatever he considered his duty to guard.

A few things are known about Owney. As a puppy, he apparently appeared out of nowhere on a cold autumn evening in 1888 at the Albany, New York, post office. No one saw him enter or even noticed him sleeping on a pile of mail bags until the following morning.

The mail clerks who found him were enchanted by the puppy's friendliness and alert bright eyes. The men talked it over and decided to "adopt" him. After all, they could take him to the Humane Society if he became troublesome. They fed him, watered him, gave him companionship and a place to sleep. As the days passed, no one came to claim Owney. Meanwhile, the men became more and more attached to the dog. He was never a problem for them, but he was definitely more of a mail bag dog than a people dog. He continued to love the mail bags, and it was this love that determined his activities, making him both adventurous and famous.

While Owney was growing up, he liked to ride on top of the mail pouches when they were taken by wagon from the post office to the railroad station. As he grew older, he branched out. He went from riding the mail wagons to riding the mail trains, leaving the Albany, New York, train station and arriving wherever the train happened to be going. In those days, railway mail cars featured stacked bins where the mail clerks would sort mail while they were riding the trains to various destinations.

Owney went to New York City on his first rail ride. As with the wagons, he rode on top of the mail bags. Soon after this trip, he started to be gone for days, returning atop a pile of mail pouches which were loaded on the wagon going from the Albany train depot to the Albany post office. While Owney always returned, the post office clerks worried that Owney might get into trouble or get lost out on his own, so they bought him a collar which read, "Owney, Post Office, Albany, New York," hoping that this would assure that he would always be sent back to the nearest place he called home. As time went on, Owney would often be gone for months. During his travels, he either spent his time lying on mail bags or looking out the door of the mail car as the train chugged along through the countryside. When

Owney wanted either a change in companionship or scenery, he would simply jump off one mail train and hop on another at the first stop.

Owney seemed to feel responsible for guarding mail. In one instance, Owney jumped on a mail wagon after the mail was loaded for the post office, but he was not on the wagon when it arrived at its destination. As the mail clerks unloaded the wagon, they found a bag missing. They immediately sent the wagon driver back to retrace his route, hoping to find the mail bag. About a mile from the depot, the driver spotted Owney sitting on the missing mail bag in a gutter where it had fallen off the wagon. He wagged his tail with delight when he was found doing his self-appointed task.

Stories like this began to appear in newspapers all over the United States and even Canada. In short order, Owney was no longer the mascot of just the Albany post office; he became the companion of railway mail clerks all over the country. He was always well cared for. James Bruns reports, "The railway mail clerks loved having Owney aboard and they made sure that he was warm, safe, and well fed. They treated him like one of the crew."

The Albany postal clerks became more and more curious about where Owney went during his increasingly long absences. Hoping to get some information, they attached a note on his collar asking others to indicate the places where he had been seen. In order to accomplish this, they asked that all employees of the Railway Mail Service record each journey by attaching an identifying metal mailbag tag to his collar. They eventually called these tags, "Owney's trinkets." It was not long before Owney had so many tags that he could hardly hold his head up. For his comfort, some tags were removed, but all the tags were always sent back to the Albany post office where the mail clerks collected and saved them. His collection of destination tags became very impressive. Eventually, the number of tags became so impressive that the Postmaster General (John Wanamaker) presented Owney with a specially designed harness, worn much like a backpack, to allow for better weight distribution of his jingling trinkets. Thus, he could wear them more comfortably.

Not all of Owney's tags were mail tags. Some tags expressed special appreciation of his courage or a love for his way of life. Some read, "Good Luck," "Owney, call again," and "To his dogship." Other tags were actual tokens of credit for such things as a drink, a cigar, a loaf of bread, or a quart of milk. These too were signs of appreciation for this dog's spunk and companionship. Owney certainly never found himself needing food or drink regardless of how far he travelled or where he found himself.

The list of Owney's destinations is endless. However, just a few examples show the broad range of his travels. He had tags from towns in Kentucky, Massachusetts, Michigan, Iowa, Minnesota, Ohio, Illinois, Washington, California and Nevada.

As Owney branched out, he returned to Albany less often, but the Albany post office always remained his home base. Everyone across the country knew this, so the Albany postal clerks were usually the first to know if Owney was in trouble. Like so many of these independent, ownerless dogs, the matter of a license seems to become an issue at least once in their lifetimes.

When Owney arrived at the Montreal, Canada, train depot, he was taken into custody because he had no license and he had no human companion. The Canadian officials, therefore, contacted the Albany post office where employees raised enough money to release him from custody and to pay for his food and lodging during his confinement. Interestingly, Owney did have dog licenses (some honorary and some paid for by volunteers) from Brooklyn, New York; Sidney, Nebraska; Sumas, Washington; and Grand Forks, South Dakota. In each of these places, someone had simply attached a license to his collar. The total number of tags, tokens, charms, trinkets, and medals pinned on Owney during his life numbered 1,017!

Not only postal clerks but newspapers around the country kept track of this dog. And it is no wonder. One day in 1896, 300 people appeared at the Brattleboro, Vermont, post office to welcome Owney to town. He once was a guest at an annual convention of the National Republican League when it was held in Buffalo, New

York. He appeared at the Iowa Bankers' Association Convention in Council Bluffs, Iowa, in 1893, and in 1895, he attended the Tacoma Poultry Association meeting in the state of Washington. He certainly did no more than wag his tail on these occasions, but the appeal of his courage, curiosity, independence, and the jingling sound of his trinkets captured the hearts of everyone who knew about him.

As he grew older, his later trips became even more remarkable. His most famous trip was in 1895. On August 19, 1895, he boarded the steamship Victoria in Tacoma, Washington, and went around the world. For some reason, the mail clerks sent him by registered mail on certain segments of this trip abroad. Using registered mail created a problem because it required that each piece of mail fit into a designated category. What to call Owney? Eventually, the mail officials created a special category just for Owney, "Registered Dog Package."

Owney chased rats aboard the ships where crews considered him a fine rat catcher. When Owney arrived in Japan, he truly baffled the officials. His grand collection of tags (decorations?) led to the belief that he belonged to a very important person. Not wishing to offend anyone of importance, Owney was given an imperial passport. This unusual (for a dog) document allowed Owney to travel unrestricted anywhere in Japan. The only restrictions were that he could not rent a house, hire a carriage without headlights at night, or scribble on public buildings and temples. Owney seemed quite able to abide by their rules.

Some weeks later, a Mr. Herbert Flood of San Francisco booked passage on a freighter out of Kobe, Japan. When he inquired if there were any other passengers on the freighter, he was told that the only other listed passenger was a Mr. Owney whose residence was in the United States. Mr. Flood asked to be introduced to Mr. Owney, and was astonished to see the clerk whistle a large Irish terrier off a pile of mail bags.

Owney's incredible trip included China, Singapore, Suez, Algiers, and the Azores. There always seemed to be someone who expected his arrival as well as someone willing to show him around an unfamiliar place. After many months, Owney ultimately arrived in New York City on the Port Phillip, a British steamer. To complete Owney's trip around the world, the New York postal clerks then sent him on a mail train back to Tacoma where he began his trip. On December 29, 1895, Owney arrived in Tacoma. Hundreds of people were at the train station to greet him. His entire trip took 132 days and was estimated to have been over 143,000 miles.

There were many newspaper stories about Owney.

Some were true, some were half-true, and some were completely false. For example, it was reported at one point that Owney had been run over and killed by a streetcar when he was, in fact, very much alive. Another story said he had lost an ear in a dog fight and a leg from being run over by a train. The latter stories were considered utter nonsense because he always appeared to be completely intact physically. Years after his death, however, it was discoverred that at least one of these stories was a half-truth.

Owney appealed to all kinds of dog lovers. Because of his exceptional life, he recieved many awards. He even received awards from prestigious dog shows, not, of course, for his breed, but for his spunk and courage. One Los Angeles kennel club gave him a silver medal for being the "best-traveled dog" at their 1893 show. At a dog show in Grand Rapids, Michigan, he was awarded a medal engraved "Owney, the Globe Trotter." He received a similar medal in Chicago.

On Owney's last trip, he went to California. He was brought on stage for the San Francisco convention of the National Association of Railway Clerks. He received a roaring, fifteen-minute display of affection. The men cheered, whistled, and clapped for this delightful travel companion who had brought so much pleasure to hundreds of mail clerks, many of whom were in the audience on this occasion. It was not only a tribute to Owney but to all the men who had watched out for him. They were proud of Owney and of themselves.

Owney had one other reputation, but superstition made the mail clerks hesitate to mention it. Owney seemed to be a good luck charm. Mail trains often met with serious accidents—derailments, collisions, and explosions. In 1893, there were more than 400 such accidents involving the deaths of many mail clerks. However, there was never an accident on any train when Owney was on board. Because of this, he became the mail clerk's good luck friend as well as their companion.

By 1897, Owney had lost the sight in one eye, he could only tolerate soft foods and milk, and it was no longer possible for him to get on and off mail trains on his own. For his welfare, he was sent to the Albany post office where his care was assured. Unfortunately, retirement did not suit him. One day Owney slipped away and managed to get on a mail train headed for Toledo.

When he arrived there, there was some kind of altercation. Owney was apparently mistreated by someone while he was being shown to a newspaper reporter. Owney apparently became angry enough to bite a postal worker. Owney died of a gunshot wound on June 11, 1897 in Toledo. All the facts of this incident were never revealed or fully explained.

Almost immediately after James White, superintendent of the railway mail service, heard of Owney's death, he organized the postal clerks in the United States. They very quickly raised enough money to hire a Toledo taxidermist to preserve Owney. Interestingly, a recent examination by historians revealed that a right ear and a right rear paw had been replaced by a taxidermist sometime between 1897 and when he was given to the Smithsonian Institution. While these exact injuries had never been reported, it does appear that some of the old rumors had a grain of truth.

Owney was first displayed at the United States Post Office headquarters in Washington, D.C. In 1911, he was given to the Smithsonian Institution. This organization continues to care for him at the National Postal Museum which the Smithsonian opened in 1993. It is here that visitors can see Owney and enjoy looking at his many trinkets, coins, medals, and mementos from the journeys of this fascinating globe trotter.

Patsy Ann

Official Greeter of Juneau, Alaska

On October 12, 1929, a litter of pure white pedigreed English bull terriers was born in Portland, Oregon. Soon after this event, Dr. Keyser, a dentist whose home was Juneau, Alaska, happened to be visiting Portland. By coincidence, Dr. Keyser was hoping to find a puppy while he was in Oregon as a surprise for his children. He was delighted when someone told him about the litter of white pedigreed English bull terriers. Dr. Keyser was very knowledgeable about dogs so when he went to see the puppies, he carefully looked over all of them. He found himself constantly returning to one of the female puppies. She seemed especially alert and interested in her surroundings. He bought that puppy and took her home to Juneau for his two daughters, Esther and Elizabeth. They named the puppy Patsy Ann.

Why did the Summer 1992 issue of *The Bull Terrier* devote its centerfold (space reserved for highly prized show dogs) to this dog on the fiftieth anniversary of her death? This was a dog who had earned fame and honor because of her deeds, rather than blue ribbons (although she had a distinguished ancestry). She had had a special relationship with the city of Juneau, remembered clearly by the old-timers but, for some reason it took 50 years for her story to become more widespread.

Patsy Ann was named for her mother, but her spirit

and temperament were probably more like that of her father whose name was Gay Diablo (happy devil). Bull terriers are a peculiar-looking breed. Some people don't even think they look like dogs. Their large heads, slanty eyes, and lean muscular bodies look like no other canine. Spuds McKensey, with his one black eye, has brought attention and stature to the breed in recent years.

Patsy Ann explored her world enthusiastically without fear, and she eventually found for herself a life that made her happy. The people of Juneau had the good sense to let her become what was right for her. This independent dog rejected all owners, overcame physical obstacles, watched for and greeted ships at Juneau's docks, enjoyed taverns and consorted with a lot of tough characters who became the friends who watched out for her. Ultimately she earned a special place in Juneau's history.

When Dr. Keyser brought his cute wiggling puppy home, she was constantly agitated and quite incorrigible. The only time she seemed to settle down was when she was sleeping. The family thought maybe she would grow out of it. Ultimately, however, Patsy Ann's inability to learn acceptable behavior created such a strain between the dog and the family, they decided to give her away.

Regretfully, the Keysers gave her to a neighbor, Dean Rice, who wanted to try his hand with this puppy. He thought that perhaps Patsy Ann would work out better with the help of his two young sons. They tried everything, but Patsy Ann continued to have other ideas. She was like a wild bronco before it is broken. She disliked being confined in any way. When she was tied up, she would strain at her leash until she broke free to run wherever she wanted. If she was fenced in, she would go either under it or over it. When she was loose, she seemed to be restlessly looking for something. The first discovery Patsy Ann found pleasurable was the school yard when it was full of the town's children playing. Their energy seemed to match hers. As she explored the town, she discovered lots of other interesting things. The boat docks were of special interest.

When she was several months old, the Keysers and the Rices realized one of Patsy Ann's problems—she was stone deaf. This may have been one of the reasons she was so easily frustrated and anxious to use her other senses, particularly smell and vision. Her deafness seemed to have a profound effect on her view of the world. Ultimately, she left the Rice home to take up residence near the boat docks where her love of boats became a lifetime passion.

Patsy Ann, like Boozer, made friends easily. She always found people who kept an eye out for her welfare.

She never wanted for food. The City Cafe was a daily stop and was probably where she regularly had her main meal, thanks to the owners. The spilled popcorn and peanuts at the Imperial Saloon were always a nice afternoon snack. In addition to these places of business, she had individual friends who slipped her other snacks and candy as she made her rounds.

She never wanted for a place to stay either. She would toast her paws next to the pot-bellied stove at the Alaska Empire Hotel in the winter and stop at other places she fancied. Her favorite place to stay, however, was the longshoremen's hall. She seemed to like people who liked what she liked—the sea, the docks, and the ships. Even the most disreputable of these men watched out for Patsy Ann.

Once Patsy Ann was free of any owners, she started to take personal responsibility for announcing the arrival of ships coming to Juneau. The port of Juneau is surrounded by islands obstructing the view of the sea. Before anyone heard a whistle blow, before any waves started to wash ashore, and before a ship could be seen (often more than a half mile away), Patsy Ann ran to the pier of Gastineau Channel, and watched and waited until the ship could be seen and heard. No one ever understood how she sensed a ship was coming. That was Patsy Ann's secret. There was speculation that perhaps she felt some ground vibration from a ship's engines in the water. It does not really matter how she did it. What is important is that she always knew when a ship was coming long before any person did.

She became a great hit with tourists. The crews on cruise ships would alert the passengers that Patsy Ann would be at the dock to greet them. In those days, it was said that she was the most photographed dog in North

America (and that included Rin Tin Tin!). Of course, tourists were also a grand source of treats and attention.

Patsy Ann was very precise about her landing announcements. She did not just know when a boat was coming, she also knew at which dock a boat would tie up. This was even more incomprehensible. On one occasion she is reported to have been waiting with a crowd for a government ship. Suddenly, she trotted over to a different dock which turned out to be the one where the boat eventually landed. This uncanny accuracy left the crowd scratching their collective heads.

Patsy Ann's dignity, a quality of her breed, was one of her strongest personal attributes. She was also very possessive about her territory. She made it clear to other dogs that the pier was her turf. However, when age and arthritis slowed her down, she no longer used her energy for such foolish shows of self-importance. Besides, it was no longer necessary. After all, by then she was Juneau's "official greeter," a title given her by Juneau's Mayor Goldstein in 1934.

Patsy Ann loved crowds. This love seemed to start with her visits to the school yard. Her love of crowds not only brought her a lot of attention, but sometimes it resulted in a good game. She was always reinforced in her love of crowds by admiring town folk, tourists and crews coming from the ships. But where were the crowds when there was no action on the docks? Some days a crowd was hard to find, but not during the baseball season. She liked to engage in the game whether she was wanted or not. On one occasion, she stopped a tie game by taking the ball from the pitcher. This was great fun because it resulted in a good chase. When she got tired and needed a rest, she gave up the ball and watched the game from the stands with the crowd.

The only time Patsy Ann seemed to get in legal trouble was in 1934 when the city passed an ordinance requiring all dogs to be licensed. It was a short skirmish with the law, however. With so many friends, she not only ended up with a fully paid license but even received a red collar on which the license was displayed.

The local newspaper regularly reported her activities and Carl Burrows published a little booklet, *Patsy Ann*, in 1939. He said, "All of us may well learn a valuable lesson from the example set by her simple devotion and faithfulness to duty as Boat Greeter of Juneau, Alaska. Patsy Ann has not sought fame, but fame has come to her. Nor has she sought worldly goods, yet she never lacks for food or a place in which to sleep. But she has sought the friendship of all human beings and far more important than fame, has gained the love and respect of the people of Juneau, and occupies an enviable place in the hearts of all who know her." The book ended, "May she live forever." Little did Mr. Burrows know what would happen many years later.

On the evening of March 30, 1942, 13 year-old Patsy Ann died peacefully in her sleep. At 12:30 PM the following day, her friends placed her in a coffin and lowered it into the waters of Gastineau Channel which she had so faithfully watched over for the past years. Many town people were there to say goodbye.

Those who loved her never forgot her. It is surprising that it took 50 years, but in 1992, the efforts of the Gastineau Humane Society and a group of citizens calling themselves "The Friends of Patsy Ann" proposed that the Alaska legislature pass a citation in her honor. The legislature passed the citation which read:

"The seventeenth Alaska State Legislature takes great enjoyment in recognizing the contribution of

Patsy Ann, 'Official Boat Greeter of Juneau, Alaska.' She did not seek fame, only to bestow friendly greetings to all she encountered—a job she undertook with dignity, persistence and single-minded dedication. Fame found her on its own.

"Born totally deaf, she nevertheless anticipated not only the arrival of all incoming steamships, but also at which of Juneau's docks they would be tying up. Cynics surmised she was attracted by the occasional morsels of food tossed through the portholes by kind-hearted travelers; but the truth was, she loved people. The bigger the crowd, the better. Baseball games were favorites; her penchant for charging the field and absconding with the ball earned equal amounts of players' ire and spectators' delight.

"Patsy Ann was as much a fixture of beer parlors and hotel lobbies as any paying guest. She was pointed out by cab drivers and photographed by tourists. Her image adorned postcards sold by curio shops. She even appeared in a talent minstrel show for which she endured the humiliation of a bath.

"Her distinctive gait slowed over the years due to rheumatism brought on by unscheduled dives into the cold water of the Gastineau Channel. Still, she always headed for the docks on the double whenever steamship whistles shook Juneau's boardwalks. Human Alaskans will forever hold Patsy Ann's name dear — longer, certainly, than those of many so-called bipeds amongst them."

The Gastineau Humane Society and Friends of Patsy Ann set up a trust and raised money for a bronze replica of Patsy Ann. From old photographs and drawings, Anna Harris, a fine sculptor, created what she calls a "spirit piece." Clippings of dog hair from around the world were placed in the bronze at the time of casting to unite the spirit of dogs everywhere. The Chidoni Foundry in New Mexico cast the model sculpted by Ms. Harris. It stands 35 inches high and is about 15 percent larger than life-size.

The bronze statue was placed on the wharf next to the flower beds in the middle of Patsy Ann Welcome Square at the waterfront in Marine Park. This life-like statue looks expectantly out over the channel just as Patsy Ann did during her life. A medicine man blessed the sculpture in the "name of harmony and the spirit of friendship between humans and animals with the prayer that it will carry over to humans in their relations with each other."

On July 3, 1992, the Alaska Princess Cruise Lines held a gala reception on their huge flagship, Regal Princess. After the reception, the statue was unveiled. If you go to Juneau, you will see the statue of Patsy Ann looking out toward the sea when you arrive at the dock. The people of Juneau ask that you "greet her and touch her and in leaving, carry with you the blessings of friendship through your life's journey." No one could ask for a finer legacy.

Weela

A Community Hero

If you drove up the road leading to the Watkins'
ranch near Imperial Beach, California in 1994, you
would have been greeted by a remarkable dog
named Weela, a 65-pound, female American pit bull
terrier. Officially an American Staffordshire terrier, and
sometimes known as a Yankee terrier, the pit bull's
unfortunate reputation comes from the men who took
advantage of the breed's rare courage by training them to

be bloody, fighting tools for unscrupulous gamblers. Without such training, an American pit bull terrier is intelligent, easily trained, strongly attached to its owner, and guardian of its owner's property. The American Pit Bull is often called "the most courageous animal ever born."

Weela was never taught to fight, nor was she harshly disciplined, so her behavior contrasts sharply with the pit bull's stereotypic reputation for viciousness. Weela was brought up surrounded by an affectionate family who taught her basic obedience and good manners. She was allowed to examine her world of animals and humans without undue restraint. She lived as an ordinary loving and beloved family pet, but her life was anything but ordinary. It was as if Weela had her own destiny and reason for being from the start.

One of ten puppies abandoned and left to die in a

back alley in Imperial Beach, California, Weela's start in life was precarious. A near tragedy was averted by a chance encounter. Good fortune came to these puppies when Lori Watkins, an animal lover, happened to go to town to do some errands the day after the puppies were abandoned. Lori parked her car and started her errands, walking several bocks, stopping at the drug store, bakery, and dry cleaners. As she walked past an alley she heard some strange sounds. They were not very loud, but they sounded like the wimpering of an animal or animals in distress. After she finished her errands, she walked back to the alley. She entered the alley and walked slowly in the direction of the sound to investigate its source. Lori was astonished to find a litter of ten puppies, apparently abandoned by both the mother and the mother's owner. She later found out that the puppies' mother was a very young American pit bull terrier that had been bred too young. When the owner discovered that the young mother, almost a puppy herself, was inadequate for her job, the owner decided to get rid of the puppies.

Once Lorie discovered the source of the strange sounds, she hurriedly carried her purchases back to her car and drove straight to the alley where the puppies were huddled together crying for food and water. She gathered them up in an old car blanket, put them in a carton she had in the back seat, and drove them home to her ranch not far from the city.

When Lori arrived home with her unusual cargo, the whole Watkins family enthusiastically pitched in and planned how to help the newest additions to their family. They fed them, watered them, played with them, kept them warm and gave them the love they so needed—the puppies had a family of human surrogate parents. It was not long before the puppies started to flourish and grow.

From the very beginning, one of the pups, a female, took a shine to the Watkins' young son. She would not let him out of her sight. She slept with him and followed him everywhere he went. In truth, this little puppy, whom they named Weela, adopted the young boy by simply claiming him as hers.

As the puppies grew older and stronger, one by one Lori found a good home for each of them—that is, all but one. Needless to say, Weela stayed on to live with the Watkins family. Finding these puppies in such a vulnerable state led to Lori's special interest in the spay/neutering program of the Humane Society.

Weela grew up to be a very happy 65-pound adult dog. She loved to run loose on the ranch, visiting with the horses, cows and chickens. She was unafraid of all but one of the animals. The only animal that baffled Weela was the goat. She was always terrified of the goat.

The family seems pretty certain that the goat never charged her. Perhaps she feared the goat because he always put his head down in a menacing way or because he had such a funny voice. No one knows. For whatever reason, Weela was always very careful to stay out of the goat's way. Weela also had her favorite animals. Her most favorite was a potbelly pig who seemed equally happy to see Weela when she came dancing and sniffing around. They sometimes seemed to have serious conversations about life and their lives in particular.

Weela also participated in all the activities of the human members of her family. She loved to swim and when the family went fishing, she was there. When the family went horseback riding up the nearby trails, Weela followed along. And when the family relaxed, she joined them on the couch, typical of most people's pets.

If Weela was such a typical pet, what made her different? In 1993, Weela became the Ken-L-Ration Dog Hero of the Year, the 40th dog so honored since the awards began in 1954. She earned this award because of the extraordinary courage she exhibited during a California flood. Weela did not just perform one act of heroism as so many other winners had, nor was her heroism solely directed toward her owners. Weela went on countless missions to rescue both strangers and animals over a period of three months. During this time she is credited with saving 30 people, 29 dogs, 13 horses, and one cat, all of whom most likely would have died during the large-scale winter flooding in southern California.

In January 1993, heavy rains caused a dam to break miles upstream on the Tijuana River. Normally a narrow, three-foot-wide river, the dam break caused wild raging waters to isolate both people and animals for almost three months. When the dam first broke through, Lori and Dan Watkins and Weela went to a neighbor's ranch to try to rescue their friend's 12 dogs. Together, they worked for six hours battling heavy rains, strong currents, and floating debris before they were able to reach the ranch to rescue the dogs. The Watkins were amazed at Weela's extraordinary ability to recognize quicksand, dangerous drop-offs, and mud bogs. She worked diligently and never let up. Both the tenaciousness and strength of her bull dog ancestors were exhibited throughout the day. Lori Watkins said, "She was constantly willing to put herself in dangerous situations. She always took the lead except to circle back if someone needed help." Weela's instinctive judgments seemed to be accurate without exception. The Watkins attributed a great deal of their success in rescuing the neighbor's dogs to Weela's efforts.

During the next month, 17 dogs and one cat were

found to be stranded on an island. On several occasions, Weela swam to the island, each time pulling 30 to 50 pounds of dog food that had been loaded into a backpack harnessed to her back. This took enormous strength as well as courage. Weela continued to provide these animals with food until they were finally evacuated on Valentine's Day.

During the peak of the flood, thirteen horses became stranded on a large manure pile where they had sought refuge from the raging waters. The frightened animals had become completely surrounded by flood waters. A rescue team used Weela to guide them through the rapidly flowing waters until all of the horses were finally brought to safe ground.

One day when Weela was returning from one of her food deliveries to stranded animals, she came upon a group of 30 people who were attempting to cross the flood waters. Weela became very excited. She refused to let them cross where they were trying to do so. She barked continuously and kept running back and forth, literally herding them to another place where it was safe to do so. Unwittingly, these people had been trying to cross the river at a point where the waters ran particularly fast and where the water was deepest. Weela knew that this was a dangerous spot, so she led them upstream to shallower water where the group was finally able to cross to the other side safely.

After several months, the Tijuana River finally became narrow and calm again. Once the emergency was over, there was no longer a need for a rescue dog, so Weela went back home to the ranch full-time to enjoy life as before. However, her community heroism was recognized. As the Ken-L-Ration's 40th award winner in their annual search for the most heroic dog in the nation, Weela received a certificate of merit, a silver-plated, engraved bowl, and a year's supply of Kibbles'n Bits dog food. Surely, the people she diverted from disaster and the animals she fed when the waters were raging around them will not forget her. Weela's life seemed to have found its purpose and destiny. However, if you saw her today running around the ranch, you would think she was just a delightful but ordinary pet.

© Peter Rains 00'

Lampo

Italy's Canine Tourist

One intolerably hot day in August, 1953, Elvio Barlettani, the assistant stationmaster at the Campilia Marittima railroad station, looked out his office window and saw a dog dart from a newly arrived freight car. He moved so quickly that Elvio questioned what he saw. The animal moved with surprising stealth and agility. Nevertherless, Elvio did not think very much about it because pet owners often ridded themselves of unwanted dogs and cats by putting them on trains going out of their town. However, this seemingly ordinary dog—medium-sized, white coated with occasional reddish brown spots—had a special air about him. He did not seem anxious or confused; in fact, he seemed to know where he was going. He ran directly to a low water fountain, took a long drink, and headed straight for the stationmaster's offices. The dog looked up at Elvio imploringly, wagged his tail, rubbed his nose against Elvio's trousers, and fell fast asleep under his desk.

Campiglia Marittima is on the west side of central Italy. It is a railroad hub for both freight and passenger trains. Nearly every train on the Turin-Rome line stops here. Campiglia is just a few miles from the port of Piombino which is on the Tyrrhenian Sea where a great many lovely summer resorts are located.

When Elvio's work shift was over, he left the dog sleeping under his desk and took his usual commuter train to his home in Piombino. His wife and four-year-old daughter, Mirna, met him at the station. Tiger, their German shepherd, was there too. On their drive home, Elvio told about the dog that had jumped off the train that afternoon. This was of special interest to Mirna who instructed her father to watch out for this unusual dog.

The next morning, Elvio took the train back to his office at Campiglia. He was not only surprised that the dog was still there, but the dog's enthusiastic greeting pleased him. His colleagues reported that the dog had refused to leave the offices during the night.

From that day forward, the dog followed Elvio every-where, including the restaurant where he had lunch regularly. The first time this happened, Elvio gave the dog a bowl of soup which was obviously appreciated. As time went on, the dog endeared himself to almost all the railroad men. They decided to give the dog a name.

They chose Lampo, which means "flash" in Italian because that's the way he had looked to Elvio when he first saw the dog as he jumped from the train at the station. Later on, they often called him Lampino to show special affection.

Lampo settled in at the railroad yards. He watched the unloading and loading of freight, investigated passengers coming and going, and always took his noon meal with someone at the local restaurant. This owner-less mongrel no longer seemed to be a typical stray.

After a couple of months, Lampo apparently decided he wanted to go home with Elvio. He was not encouraged to do so because of the rules about animals on trains. However, Lampo found his own way of sneaking onto the train without being seen. One evening, Elvio was watching the countryside as he rode home and suddenly realized that Lampo was under his seat.

This first trip to Elvio's home did not go smoothly. Mirna was ecstatic. She had heard about Lampo and knew she would like him. She adored him instantly. After supper, Tiger, the family's German shepherd, was truly out of sorts because no one had paid any attention to him. Without warning, Tiger lunged at Lampo and was definitely the victor before the family could separate them. Lampo ran out of the house and apparently caught the evening train back to Campiglia because he was there to greet Elvio upon his arrival at work the next morning.

Lampo's desire to be with Elvio's family ultimately became stronger than his fear of Tiger. Eventually, when he started going home regularly with Elvio in the evening, he would always catch an evening train back to Elvio's office where he preferred to sleep. On one occasion, Lampo took an evening walk with the family and stayed outside the theatre while his adopted family saw a movie. That night he stayed overnight because he seemed to know that the last train to Campiglia had left several hours before.

One day Elvio took Lampo to the beach for a swim. Lampo loved rolling in the sand, but appeared to be afraid of the water even when Elvio went in the water and called to him. Indeed, this so alarmed Lampo that he ran away. When Elvio started for home, he called Lampo and looked everywhere for him. Giving up, he went to his car and there was Lampo waiting for him.

Later in the summer, the Barlettani family went to the seaside for a vacation. One day as Elvio was sunning himself on the beach alone, he felt a warm, furry body brushing against him to get his attention. How Lampo had found them is a mystery. To get there, he would have had to take the train to Piombino, realize that the family's car was missing and then walk for miles along strange roads. This was one of the first occasions when Lampo demonstrated his extraordinary ability to find his way to strange places.

Lampo did one very unusual thing during that vacation. He sat on the shore for hours looking out at the sea. He seemed anxious, almost as if he was expecting someone. In spite of this, Lampo eventually learned to enjoy swimming and he especially loved riding in their rubber Zodiac boat, letting the waves rock him from side to side.

After vacation was over, Lampo went back to his routine with an additional embellishment. He would settle in for a nap in Elvio's office at two o'clock in the afternoon. Waking at three o'clock sharp, he would dash to the door and push it open with his muzzle. Then, about 15 minutes later, he would return looking very satisfied with himself.

Out of curiosity, Elvio followed him one afternoon. Lampo went straight to the platform just as the Turin-Rome express pulled in. With upturned head, he checked the train windows. When he got alongside the diner, he stopped. The cook leaned out the window and threw out some delectable bones covered with meat. He then went to the second platform where the Rome-Genoa-Turin express arrived. He again looked up and found the diner. This time he barked. Soon, the cook threw out some canine delicacies. When these trains were late, Lampo's sixth sense seemed to inform him. He always arrived at the platforms just as the trains were pulling in, regardless of what time they arrived.

Sometimes the cooks had no leftovers. Lampo became very depressed when this occurred, but he figured out how to handle these days. He started to save a few bones from days of abundance so that he would have something to eat when the cooks had no leftovers.

Once when Lampo was enjoying his afternoon handouts, a train started to pull out and the protruding step of a passenger car hit him, sending him rolling over the tracks. Ever after that experience, he carefully looked to the right and to the left whenever he crossed a track, and always chewed on his meaty bones well away from the rails.

Lampo frequently arranged his travel schedule so that he would be in Piombino in the morning in order to escort Mirna to kindergarten and again in the afternoon to escort her home. He was beginning to enjoy travel more and more, but he always knew the train schedules so that he could perform his self-appointed duties.

One summer, Mirna went to visit her grandmother up in the hills. When it came time for her to return home, Lampo, Elvio, and his wife drove up into the hills to fetch her. They stopped at a little church on the way up the hill to offer a special prayer of thanks for their good life. While the family was engaged in prayer, they became aware that the sexton was yelling and chasing Lampo with a broom. When they returned to their car, Lampo was nowhere. They searched and called their beloved Lampino but there was no response. Reluctantly, they continued on to the grandmother's house where they spent the night. Everyone was distraught. They were sure Lampo would get lost in the unfamiliar hills. The trip home the next day started in a somber mood. As they crossed a little country road, they spotted a white object up ahead. It was Lampino. They greeted him with tears of joy. Elvio checked his odometer. The dog had discovered the family's route after travelling unfamiliar roads for fifteen miles!

Lampo had always exhibited a certain restlessness

from time to time. He loved the family he had adopted, but he apparently wanted more. He started checking out passenger trains from the engine to the last car. He always stayed away from freight trains, however. After checking each car, he would jump up on the first step, then jump off when the train started to move. Finally, one day he jumped onto the first step, but did not jump off when the train went off to Rome. The first time it happened, the Barlettanis were terrified. Lampo was gone for two days. However, on Monday morning he was at the Barlettani's front door ready to escort Mirna to school.

By now, Lampo was quite famous. All of the railroad men knew him. Passengers always looked for him when they travelled his routes. The Italian newspapers printed many stories about him. No one understood how he knew what train went where and when, so people started to make up humorous explanations. Some said he learned to read train schedules. Others said he learned to count so he could recognize train numbers. Maybe he was psychic or clairvoyant. Scent certainly did not explain all of it. Elvio decided that Lampo learned that if he left in one direction, he could get back by going in the opposite direction. However, this theory did not explain how he could be seen in Florence as well as in small, unimportant stations in every direction. Lampo could simply go in any direction and still find his way home whether it was on an express or a milk train.

During the height of his first travel days, Lampo had a free pass to almost anywhere because the station personnel enjoyed watching him so much. After some time, however, a few people complained. Some even hampered his efforts to get on the trains he wanted to ride. Lampo had an excellent memory and he was stubborn, irritable, and perhaps even spiteful. He remembered those who had thwarted his efforts, and he would growl ferociously when he met up with them at a later time. For example, he never forgave an old engineer who took his picture with a flash bulb.

Eventually, there were so many unsettling incidents that Elvio decided to bring Lampo back to his home for a cooling off period. It took a while for Tiger and Lampo to coexist without rancor, but they both learned the art of ignoring each other. Tiger had a particularly tough time. He ate dog food while Lampo ate meat and bones (because Lampo refused to eat at all unless he had his usual menu). Lampo chose to be an aggressive guard dog for the Barlettanis. In fact, the grocer, the baker, and the milkman stopped making deliveries to their house.

Lampo appeared to adjust very well to family living with the Barlettanis. However, he continued to be restless when he heard the trains pass and whistles blow at crossroads. The cooks, the trainmen, and many passengers truly missed him. Finally, Elvio decided to try to let him go back to the station although he also tried to curtail the amount of his travel.

This worked until a new station master was appointed. He was stern, abided by the rules, and was going to have none of Lampo. The new boss called Elvio into his office privately. "The dog must go. Either you get rid of him or I will have the dogcatcher remove him."

Elvio was beside himself as were many of the employees. Lampo needed his freedom. Certainly, they could not keep him tied up in a yard. The men finally agreed to send Lampo away in the same manner he had arrived—on a freight train. They put him on a train that was going non-stop as far south as possible. Everyone came to the station to say goodbye to Lampo, who looked very bewildered as someone restrained him from jumping off the train. *This* trip was not his idea.

Worried about his welfare, Elvio called around to the train stations. No one had seen Lampo or heard anything about him. Every night when Elvio arrived home, Mirna asked if he had any news of her Lampino. Winter was coming on, and both the weather and the mood was grim. As time went on, Mirna stopped asking about Lampo and Elvio assumed that she had finally forgotten about him. But one night as he passed Mirna's room, he heard her crying and asking God to bring Lampino back.

The long cold winter was finally over, and spring brought the blossoms of the almond and peach trees. Elvio and his wife had agreed to find a puppy who would be named Lampo for Mirna. One afternoon, as Elvio was working on the railroad books, he heard a loud commotion outside. One of the men ran into his office and shouted, "Come quick!" Elvio ran outside and stopped in his tracks as he saw a thin dog, wagging his tail ever so slowly, looking out from dark, suffering eyes. While he was terribly changed, there was no doubt it was Lampo. Elvio scooped him up in his arms and told him they would never send him away again. Elvio's tears were of guilt, joy, and relief. The men rejoiced with him. Even the stationmaster came by to pat Lampo. Then he turned to Elvio and said, "Look after him, get him well, and he can stay here with us from now on."

They gave Lampo some warm milk and he fell asleep under Elvio's desk. He slept fitfully. Sometimes his whole body trembled. No one knew what he had gone through, but his battered body clearly showed he had suffered a great deal. When Elvio left for home, Lampo was still fast asleep.

The word had spread through town before Elvio had

a chance to tell of the homecoming. Mirna ran to her father as he walked into the yard. "Lampo is back. I don't want any other dog but my Lampino."

When Elvio arrived at the office the next day, Lampo was unable to get up to greet him, but he wagged his tail for him. The men were concerned; Lampo would not eat. Later in the day, when a train with a dining car pulled in, Lampo tried to get up, but he couldn't. He tried to take milk for Elvio, but he just could not swallow.

Elvio decided to take Lampo home for the night. Mirna did not even recognize him. When she did, she sobbed. The veterinarian came to the house and examined Lampo. He said there was nothing he could do, that the dog had suffered too much, and he had a serious intestinal infection. He added that the dog had only a few more hours to live.

The Barlettanis stayed with the dog all that night. He

was very quiet, too quiet, but suddenly, Lampo staggered up and started toward the door. It was clear that he wanted to die at the Campiglia station. Elvio, his wife, and Mirna put Lampo in the car and drove him to the station. They put him under Elvio's desk and said tearful goodbyes. Lampo looked at them gratefully, and they departed.

When Elvio's train pulled into Campiglia the next morning, he expected bad news from the men. However, his office door stood open with Lampo standing up to greet him. Elvio rushed off to get him some warm milk which was taken enthusiastically. Lampino was obviously much better, but they were not convinced he would be well until he went to the diner of the Rome train at precisely three o'clock.

Lampo started to pick up his duties as before, escorting Mirna to and from school, riding the local trains to and from Campiglia and Piombino. No one ever learned just where he had been or what he had gone through. Nonetheless, Elvio pieced some information together. He had been seen in Barletta, 427 miles from Campiglia, and Reggio Calabria which is south of Barletta at the toe of Italy's boot, another 311 miles, for a total of 738 miles. The information was sketchy but probably fairly accurate.

Lampo's travels brought him new fame. Newspaper headlines referred to him as "Lampo the Wonder Dog," "Lampo the Railroad Dog," "Lampo the Travelling Dog," "Lampo the Express Dog," "Lampo the TV star," and "Lampo on video." The American magazine *This Week* devoted three pages to Lampo in 1960. Through it all, Lampo still charged anyone who put a flash bulb in his face, but he did take to the interviews with great dignity and possibly even a little pleasure.

Amidst all of this publicity, Campiglia was about to get a new stationmaster. The old chief had to retire. As he left the station for the last time, he leaned down and said something to Lampo, but Lampo gave no response. He knew who had sent him on that terrible journey. Rumors were rife. Would the new man like dogs? If so, how strict would he be about the rules? What about Lampo?

Finally, it was announced. The new stationmaster was a dog lover. On his first day on the job, he came up to Elvio and said, "I hear you're Lampo's favorite. Where is he? I want to meet him." Lampo was on a trip at the moment, but later in the afternoon he returned. When he saw the new boss, he curled his lip and looked very menacing, but he apparently gave it a second thought because he began to sniff the man's shoes and trousers. Soon Lampo gave his approval with an enthusiastic wag of the tail.

During the next summer, a short, old man with a bushy white beard entered the station to get a ticket to Leghorn. As he waited for his train, he took a turn around the station grounds. When he saw Lampo, he went up to him and spoke to him. Lampo sniffed him and then became very excited about seeing him.

Elvio noticed this exchange and went out to talk to the man. "Was this dog ever yours?" he asked.

The man then told the story of an American sailor who owned Bigheri (Lampo's name then). When the sailor's ship was to leave, he could not find his dog. While sympathetic, the captain said the ship had to leave on time. Soon after the ship departed, the dog came to the dock, but too late to get on board. For weeks afterward, the dog would sit on the pier and look out at sea. This explained Elvio's observations whenever Lampo went to the beach. The old man had taken care of the dog for almost a year after the sailor left, but one day Bigheri went to the train station and was never seen again.

The old man was very wistful and asked to have the dog back if at all possible. Elvio said, "Let the dog decide." When the old man boarded his train to Leghorn, Lampo went with him. Four days later, he was back at the station, but Lampo returned to visit the old man on several other occasions before the old man died.

As Lampo's age and failing health curtailed his travels, he could no longer jump on and off trains, but the Campiglia station remained his home. The new stationmaster made it clear that it would remain his home as long as he lived and he promised to have Lampo buried under the acacia tree nearby.

Lampo continued to enjoy lying between tracks two and three to watch the action. Occasionally, Elvio would bring him home for the night, but he always brought him back to his favorite place, the station. Late one summer afternoon, Lampo apparently misjudged his position near a track because of his failing eyes. He slipped under a train. The men were stricken. Elvio could not look. The boss was called. Too distraught to come, the boss had the men bury Lampino under the acacia tree near the station.

No one who had ever known Lampo would ever forget his independence or his loyalty. But most of all, no one would ever fathom his ability to go wherever he wanted and to find any place he was looking for. This was his secret, and he revealed it to no one. Lampo's life and courageous adventures won many hearts in his adopted country, Italy.

Old Drum

Burden vs. Hornby Becomes
A Community Cause

One cold October evening in 1869, Charles
Burden, a Missouri farmer, walked to a nearby
farm to visit a friend. He brought along his
hunting hounds in case he decided to do some hunting
on his way back home later in the evening. After dinner,
the two friends sat on porch rockers and chatted. Out in
the fields, both men's dogs bayed at the night animals,

the moon and the stars. Some folks say a coonhound's voice is as sweet and melodious as a bugle call.

The two men listened with pride. They were able to identify the distinctive voice of each of their dogs. Charles Burden especially enjoyed hearing Drum's voice because it was so clear. Drum was special. He had wandered onto Burden's farm several years before and stayed, much to the satisfaction of both Burden and Drum who turned out to be a fine coon dog. Old Drum, as he was often called, became Burden's favorite dog as well as his constant companion. He was also the best hunter Charlie Burden had ever had. That probably meant that Old Drum was an excellent night hunter, treeing only coons and no trash (animals other than coons). To this day, that is the definition of a good hound—one that hunts by scent rather than sight.

Anyone who had ever hunted with Drum agreed that

he was the best. In 1869 such animals were badly needed because many people needed to hunt in order to put meat on their tables. This made a good hunting dog very valuable, even necessary.

As the two men talked, a shot rang out from Lon Hornsby's place which adjoined Burden's farm. Suddenly the hounds were silent. Fearing the worst, the two friends jumped up, found their hunting horns, and immediately called in their hounds. One by one, they all came running from several directions toward the sound of the horns, except for Drum.

Charles Burden had a sickening hunch that Old Drum was dead. He was stricken. It didn't take him long to speculate what might have happened. While he had never had any overt trouble with Lon Hornsby, his brother-in-law, he knew he could anger quickly. First, Lon had been losing sheep. He really did not know what animal was killing them, but he blamed it on dogs, and he had sworn he would shoot the first dog he saw on his place. Besides Lon Hornsby's violent temper, Burden also knew that Lon was bringing up a twelve-year-old boy named Dick Ferguson who did whatever Lon told him to do.

Burden left his friend's house feeling very sad at the almost certain loss of both his good companion and his good hunter. He waited until dawn the next day to visit Lon who lived next door. As he walked into Lon's yard, he found Lon working the soil for planting corn. The two men exchanged a quick hello. Burden came straight to the point. He asked if Lon had seen Drum around the previous night. After an evasive answer, Burden then asked about the gun shot that he and his friend had heard. Hornsby denied knowing anything about either matter. After a few minutes, however, Lon did say that

Dick Ferguson had shot at a dog prowling around the yard. Then he pointed to a cedar tree at the edge of the yard and a trail where the dog had supposedly run off.

Burden walked over to the cedar tree and looked around at the ground. He was immediately suspicious because there were no signs of blood anywhere. He decided to investigate further. He walked across the farm fields searching the banks of Big Creek. Finally, he discovered Drum lying in shallow water, just a few miles from his own farm. He was, of course, dead. As Burden examined Old Drum's body, he became incensed with what he surmised had happened. Drum had been shot with mixed shot producing varying-sized holes in his body. He also found sorrel hair (brownish-colored horse hairs) under the dog. That, along with the mud and the direction of the dog's coat, seemed to be almost certain evidence that Drum had been dragged to the creek.

Charles Burden wanted justice. He had lost his friend and favorite hunting dog. His brother-in-law not only owned sorrel horses but he had lied to him about the circumstances of the dog's death. What really bothered Burden was that his Old Drum had died falsely accused of being a "sheep killer." He went to town and filed a suit against Hornsby for murdering his dog. This started a series of four trials and three appeals. The case of Burden vs. Hornsby lasted for several years. Old Drum's death became a cause. His owner had great courage, faith in his dog, and a determination to exonerate his dog with the help of a brilliant young attorney.

The arguments used by both sides were fairly similar in all of the trials. Hornsby claimed there was nothing but circumstantial evidence against him. Burden claimed it was a deliberate murder based on Hornsby's vow that he would kill the first dog he saw on his property because of the loss of his sheep. Hornsby's sorrel mule figured prominently in the evidence presented by Burden's lawyers.

At the first trial, the jury could not come to any agreement. By this time, the people in all the towns surrounding Warrensburg, Missouri, started to take sides. Even dog lovers and dog owners did not always agree. Quite a few of the men in town had hunted with Old Drum and they knew him to be a fine, reliable dog. Their word was especially influential. It seemed as if the majority of people were on Burden's side.

With no judgment in the first trial, Burden changed lawyers, appealed and was granted a second trial. At the second trial, Hornsby was ordered to pay Burden twenty-five dollars. Angry, Hornsby took his case to the next highest court, suing Burden on the basis of losing because of circumstantial evidence. At this trial, Hornsby won. The people in town followed every detail of the trials. Rumors were just as important as facts. The case stimulated many lively unofficial trials and juries.

Burden was persistent. His dog's reputation was at stake, and, by this time, his own reputation was also at stake. He then sued Hornsby again, changing law firms once more.

This time Burden went to the law firm, Phillips and Vest in Sedalia, Missouri. He hired George Graham Vest. Mr. Vest was a bright young lawyer, just starting out in politics, and one who had a reputation for being an eloquent and persuasive orator. Indeed, Mr. Vest eventually served as a United States senator from Missouri for twenty-four years, having a very prestigious lifetime career. But that was quite a few years later.

After all the evidence had been presented in the fourth and last trial, Mr. Vest made his closing remarks.

His appeal was to dog owners and dog lovers. He did not once mention either Charles Burden or Old Drum in his summary statement which was as follows.

"Gentlemen of the Jury: The best friend a man has in this world may turn against him and become his enemy. His son or daughter that he has reared with loving care may prove ungrateful. Those who are nearest and dearest to us, those whom we trust with our happiness and our good name, may become traitors to their faith. The money that a man has, he may lose. It flies away from him, perhaps when he needs it the most. A man's reputation may be sacrificed in a moment of ill considered action. The people who are prone to fall on their knees to do us honor when success is with us may be the first to throw the stone of malice when failure settles its cloud upon our heads. The one absolutely unselfish friend that man can have in this selfish world, the one that never deserts him and the one that never proves ungrateful or treacherous is his dog.

"Gentlemen of the Jury, a man's dog stands by him in prosperity and in poverty, in health and in sickness. He will sleep on the cold ground, where the wintry winds blow and the snow drives fiercely, if only he may be near his master's side. He will kiss the hand that has no food to offer, he will lick the wounds and sores that come in encounters with the roughness of the world. He guards the sleep of his pauper master as if he were a prince. When all other friends desert he remains. When riches take wings and reputation falls to pieces, he is as constant in his love as the sun in its journey through the heavens. If fortune drives the master forth an outcast in the world, friendless and homeless, the faithful dog asks no higher privilege than that of accompanying him to guard against danger, to fight against his enemies, and when the last scene of all comes, and death takes the master in its embrace and his body is laid away in the cold ground, no matter if all other friends pursue their way, there by his graveside will the noble dog be found, his head between his paws, his eyes sad but open in alert watchfulness, faithful and true even in death."

When Vest finished, there was silence and most eyes in the court room were teary. The jury, visibly moved, left to deliberate the findings. It reportedly took them only a few minutes to return with the verdict of guilty, awarding Burden $50 in damages. The jury also told the judge they wanted the dog killer sent to prison. However, no Missouri law existed that would allow imprisonment of a dog killer.

Hornsby was just as persistent as Burden. He made one final effort. First, he filed for a new trial. This was overruled by the court, but they did grant him an appeal to the First District Court, and allowed him to post a $1500 bond to take his case to the state Supreme Court. Ultimately the Supreme Court supported the decision of the lower court. The case finally ended on September 18, 1872, when Hornsby paid Charles Burden $50, almost three years after Old Drum had been killed. The dog's reputation was at last restored as his name was cleared of wrong doing. Charles Burden had finally satisfied his need for justice.

This is not the end of the story of Old Drum. Vest's words fired everyone's desire to pay tribute to their own special animals. While Vest's words were not recorded on the day of the trial, two persons claimed to have memorized Vest's remarks, never forgetting them. Icie Johnson's history of this event suggests that Vest's words survived the same way that folk songs, ballads, family histories and other tales survive—through telling rather than writing. Eventually, the closing argument became known as the "Eulogy to the Dog" and was published in several local newspapers. The story spread rapidly, first in the state of Missouri and then fanning out across the country to other newspapers. It has been repeated for dog lovers in every state and many foreign countries.

During the eighty years following Vest's eulogy, various citizens in the town of Warrensburg worked to make Old Drum a symbol of the bond between dogs and their owners. The old court house where the last trial took place in Warrensburg eventually became a private home. In 1914, the owner, W. O. Davis, placed a bronze tablet on the outside wall of the building. It reads, "Within these walls on Sept. 23, 1870, Senator George Graham Vest delivered his famous eulogy on the dog. He died Aug. 14, 1904 and was buried in Bellefontaine cemetery in St. Louis."

In 1947, Fred Ford placed a monument to Old Drum on Big Creek, very near the place where Charles Burden found Old Drum's body. The base of the monument contains blocks and stones from all over the world. The gray granite stone monument reads, "Killed, Old Drum, 1869," and the carving depicts a hound dog that has treed a coon in the center, a chased deer in one corner, and a chased fox in the other corner.

Then, on September 27, 1958, Warrensburg, Missouri, celebrated the dedication of yet another tribute to Old Drum. A new statue of Old Drum was unveiled in a three-hour ceremony. A dog named Butch served as the model for the statue of Old Drum. This statue stands atop the full text of Vest's Eulogy to the Dog. Senator Vest's great-granddaughter attended the parade which included several bands and assorted floats. The Boy Scouts of the Old Drum Troop 400 were in full uniform to march in the parade. A special program demonstrating obedience training and police dog exercises followed the parade. Vest's words were spoken by a local college student. Interestingly, the funds for the statue which stands in front of the new court house came from nearly every state in the U.S., as well as many foreign countries.

Old Drum's status as a community dog did not occur until many years after his death. It was his death, not his life, that made him a celebrity. And, it was really his lawyer who made him famous. This dog died over one hundred years ago yet he probably has more plaques memorializing him than any other community dog. George Vest so captured the unique nature of the emotional ties between dog owners and their dogs that it continues to strike a universal chord with anyone who has had a beloved dog.

Tricksey

A Nursing Home Dog

Although a true story, it seems better to let
Tricksey tell it in spite of the anthropomorphism
and a few minor changes in events.

It isn't easy being a nursing home dog. Few people seem to realize our special problems. There are a lot of subtle nuances that an ordinary dog doesn't have to contend with. I know because I used to be an ordinary dog. For instance, what's a nursing home dog supposed to do when a mean old man like Mr. Judkins pokes you in the ribs with his cane for no reason? Growling or snarling is out of the question because I'm a golden retriever, and that kind of behavior simply is not in our nature. I'm very proud of my golden ancestors and their reputation for friendliness and gentleness, no matter how seriously challenged they might be with people like him. Anyway, I've about made up my mind to let out a loud yip the next time he pokes me.

At the other extreme, it's also very hard to handle fairly all the nice people who love you and want to scratch you. If I let it get out of hand, I would lose a lot of fur. What room should I sleep in when four or five people want and *need* me? Where do I go when I need peace and quiet once in awhile? And all those snacks that people save from their meals! Sometimes I get so full I just have to lie down and rest. Because of all these special problems, I want to tell you my own story from the beginning.

For starters, you'll want to know how I ended up being *the* dog for the Episcopal Church Home in St. Paul, Minnesota. Well, I was told that there used to be a law against having pets live in a nursing home. That law was changed in 1984. It turns out I was kind of a pioneer in this living arrangement. Right after the law was changed, Dave, the administrator of the Episcopal Church Home, got the residents together and asked them if they might like to have a dog live there at the home. It seems they were very enthusiastic. Because most of them had pets before they moved to the home, they knew how a dog could liven things up. So, the search for just the right dog started.

They found me at the Humane Society. I was in a pretty sad state of mind because my folks had moved overseas and didn't take me with them. There I was, a one-year-old, trained golden retriever with nothing to do but pace around my kennel. They were right about my being trained, but there was a part of me that wasn't golden retriever. I know, because I remember Mom. She was blond, but she had short hair. It really wasn't important. I sure looked and acted like a golden retriever.

I suppose I better explain about my name. I started out being called Beauty. When I was young, I loved to chew things up. I didn't care whether it was a chair leg, a slipper, a pillow, a briefcase or what. I was quick to learn that the family didn't like me chewing up their things. However, it gave me real pleasure so I started thinking of ways I could stay in good with the family and still have my way. After giving this some thought, I figured if they didn't see the damaged goods, then I could enjoy myself and they'd never know the difference. So, I decided to chew up only little things that I could stash in the basement behind the furnace.

Ingenious, yes? After all it was summer time. What I didn't know was that they had the furnace cleaned in the summer. Anyway, it was great fun while it lasted. But that's when they changed my name to Tricksey.

When my family left me at the Humane Society, the two kids, Annie and Mary Jane, hugged me and kissed me all the while they were crying. I felt just awful and wondered what was going to happen to me. Two days after my family had gone, I looked out my kennel (a very demeaning situation for a proud dog who was used to being free) and saw this tall guy walking by. He caught my attention because he had long dark whiskers on his face and chin. Never had seen that before. He noticed I was staring back at him so he stopped to talk. We hit it off pretty good. They let me out of my cage so I could smell him and get a scratch. The next thing I knew, this bearded guy clipped a leash onto my collar and put me in his car. Good grief, it was scary. I didn't know what was going on. Where was he taking me?

After driving for a long time, he pulled up in front of a great big red brick building and parked his car. I looked around and took a leak as he led me into the building. *Gadzooks*, what a big family was standing in the hall as we entered. I didn't see any kids, but everyone seemed to like me fine. They said kind things and nearly everyone petted me. In return, I smelled and licked all the hands that reached out to scratch me. I figured I'd better start making friends with as many of these people as possible right away.

Not only was it a big family, but it was a huge house. Everyone lived in a different room, and there were three floors with lots of halls that seemed to keep turning a different direction everywhere I went. It took me quite a bit of time before I could go from one place to another without getting lost. It also took time to learn how the people I liked smelled compared to the ones I didn't like. Some of the first people I met were Sally (she let me out and fed me), Father Dick, Mabel the cook, and a large woman in white (Mrs. Ambrose). Then there were all those folks with canes and walkers. Some even rode around in wheelchairs. Picking and choosing my friends was not easy. I finally decided to count all the folks who regularly gave me cookies as my friends. Those who did not give me cookies did not have the pleasure of my company. Those who gave me cookies received my time and my devotion. I put on a lot of weight, but I didn't care.

My best friend was Mrs. Murphy, who invited me to her room a lot. She let me sleep in her room so I could get away from it all, and she always had a bowl of water and dog treats for me. We'd often take walks outside together, have nice chats, enjoy the flower garden and sometimes rest on a bench in the shade of a great big tree.

Those were my happiest days.

Mrs. Murphy and I got to be such good friends that I decided to always spend the night in her room. After a couple of years, I noticed Mrs. Murphy didn't want to take walks anymore and she stuck pretty much to her room even for meals. I hung around in her room more than I had because she seemed to like having me near her. She took lots of naps. Sometimes I even got up on the bed beside her. Then one day she took a nap as usual, but after some time, she didn't seem to move at all. I nudged her and gave a little moan, but she did not answer me. Something was very wrong. I ran into the hall not knowing quite what to do. Finally, I saw a nurse. I barked and whined at her until she followed me into Mrs. Murphy's room. When the nurse saw her, she covered her with a sheet and had a little tear in her eye as she gave me a hug.

I missed Mrs. Murphy something awful and grieved for a long time. As time went on, I realized I had to start making new living arrangements for myself. What should I do? I finally decided to go with Father Dick, the chaplain. He had his own office and he was very good to me. What was really good was that he visited almost everyone about two or three times a week. By following him, I got around to see everybody.

When we made our rounds together, I noticed that some people made a bigger fuss about seeing me than they did about seeing Father Dick. But he didn't seem to mind because he knew they liked each of us for different reasons. Eventually, I picked a place under his big desk for my bed. I often went to chapel and sometimes attended a memorial service.

Occasionally other dogs would come with families for a visit with someone. If I happened to be near the door when they came in, I'd growl in a deep scarey tone and then walk away. I needed to tell them not to stay! I wasn't about to share the good life with some other dog.

Everything went very well for quite a few years. Then I started having trouble with my hips—I couldn't run up and down the halls like I used to, and it often hurt to walk. I taught myself to waddle in a special way so that it didn't hurt so much. Father Dick was starting to walk funny too, something about his knees. We made quite a pair making our rounds. Sometimes we heard people laugh at us, but it was always in a loving way. It was beginning to be more and more difficult to tell us from the regular residents of the home.

I started seeing a doctor. Either Dave or Father Dick went with me. Whenever I saw the doctor, he would try new pain pills. They usually worked for a while, but it never lasted. Pretty soon I started having other problems. I got so I didn't want to eat, and that certainly was a new wrinkle for me! I began to feel kind of weak and, grudgingly, I stopped making rounds with Father Dick. I just stayed in his office, slept a lot, and only went out when I had to go.

I really missed seeing everyone, but I just felt too tired. One Friday, Father Dick picked me up, carried me to his car, and took me to the doctor again. The doc and he talked for quite a long time. All the while Father Dick was stroking me and talking to me, and saying what a good dog I had been. It was very comforting. Then, just before I went to sleep, Father Dick said, "Tricksey, you've made a lot of people very happy. You have been a very special dog, indeed."

Red Dog

Of Western Australia

R ed Dog was a free spirit who captured the love
and affection of the people in the Pilbara
region, the northern part of Western Aus-
tralia. It is a mostly harsh, sparsely populated area. In the
early 1960s, just a little over 3,000 people lived in this
316,000 square mile expanse of warm, rainy coastal
plain, rugged mountains, and desert. In the late 1960s, a
major change occurred. The Hamersley Iron Company
opened an iron ore mine at Mt. Tom Price, built a

railway track to Dampier, and built facilities for stockpiling and shipping ore for world-wide export. This was followed by development of a solar salt industry, Dampier Salt Co., on the tidal mud flats near Dampier Island. All of this required rapid development of accomodations for workers, roads and new towns. Other industries followed, including the eventual discovery and development of natural gas in the area. By 1991, 17 percent of all Australian export dollars came from products shipped out of the port of Dampier.

Red Dog started his life in 1971 when the Pilbara region was developing rapidly. His mother was a cross between a kelpie and an Australian cattle dog. A kelpie is historically a cross between a dingo (a reddish-colored wild Australian dog) and a smooth haired Scottish collie. Red Dog was one of a litter of three puppies and was first owned by a man named Colonel

Cummings who named him Tally Ho. The colonel found Tally to have a "natural wanderlust" with a "limitless supply of energy." He would sometimes drive the dog to the Paraburdoo airport (over four miles from his home), let him out of the car, and speed away. The dog would run behind the car all the way home and never seem to get tired.

When Tally was about a year old, Colonel Cummings was transferred to Dampier, over 200 miles south of his home in Paraburdoo. Because Tally had the unpleasant social habit of what the Australians call "breaking wind," he rode to Dampier, not in the family car, but in an open trailer. When the family arrived in Dampier, Tally was almost unrecognizable because he was covered with the red dust which is so characteristic of the Pilbara Region. Soon after this trip, Tally was re-named Red Dog. For the rest of his life, his reddish coat was habitually covered with the red dust of the land he travelled.

Red Dog explored his exciting new environment soon after his arrival in Dampier. He first met Hamersley Iron workers at the company quarters for single men. Next, he discovered Hamersley Iron's Transportation Section which, among other things, transported workers to and from work at the mine. The workers enjoyed the dog's inquisitive nature and kept him well fed. Soon they began to smuggle him into the repair shop. It was here that Red Dog picked out a new owner for himself. His name was John Stazzonelli, a truck driver for the iron company.

John enjoyed Red Dog and seemed to be agreeable to the adoption arrangement even though Red Dog literally shadowed him everywhere. Red would ride with John as far as Perth which was almost 4,000 miles round trip from Dampier. However, when John had a date with a girl, he would do everything to try to lose his constant companion. On one occasion, he was sure he had fooled Red Dog when he took his date to an outdoor movie. Just as the couple was settled in for the evening, Red Dog's search through all the parked cars was successful. When he found John's car, he immediately "broke wind" to emphasize his enthusiasm for this triumph.

Tragically, John was killed in a motorcycle accident on July 23, 1975. From then on, Red Dog made his way more or less alone. His way was a constant restless wandering, always keeping people at a certain emotional distance. Most folk thought he spent the rest of his life searching for John because he travelled and retravelled the outback that he had learned from John. He apparently found lady friends everywhere he went, as look-alikes started turning up in many places he visited. However, his life was very hard, so the people up and down the western side of Australia looked out for him as best they could. All the bus drivers and truckers knew him, and when they saw him, they let him hitch a ride and gave him food. Once, a new Hamersley driver, unaware of Red's privileges, refused to let him on his bus. When Hamersley workmen heard about it, they staged a protest which resulted in changing the new driver's attitude.

On one occasion, Red became separated from his driver on a trip to Perth. When the driver returned to Dampier, Red Dog was already there—a distance of about 1,000 miles! It was never possible to know how many car and truck drivers stopped and said, "Hop aboard, Red Dog" when they saw him standing by the side of the road with his muddy paw raised.

Red Dog, while a formidible scrapper when threatened, was basically a gentle soul. If any child pushed or prodded him in an unpleasant manner, he would just walk away. He simply refused to be peevish with a child. He also showed concern when he sensed that a child was ill. He often chose to stay at the side of a sick child until he or she was feeling better. Then Red Dog would return to his normal activities.

More and more people came forward to help Red Dog. Don, an electrician for Dampier Salt Company, took him in for a while after Red had fallen off the back of a truck. He even made Red a financial member of the Dampier Salt Sports and Social Club and set him up with a bank account at the Wales Bank which adopted a new slogan, "If Red banks at the Wales, you can too." Next, Don registered Red with the local shire (county). This gave him the offical title of "Dog of the North-west," allowing him to roam where he wanted to, often in places where other dogs were not tolerated.

Because the outback is so rough and desolate, Red Dog was, of course, exposed to hunters, other dogs, and many wild animals. One day, two employees of Dampier Salt heard that Red Dog had been shot near Karratha, so they went to rescue him. When they found him, they took him to the nearest veterinarian who anesthetized him, removed two bullets from his hind leg, and gave him antibiotics. The veterinarian needed to observe Red for a few hours after the surgery, so the two rescuers went to the nearest pub to pass the time. Several hours later, the rescuers returned very relaxed, got Red Dog, and started for home at high speed. On their way, a patrolman stopped them. Between the fine for speeding, the veterinarian bill, and the lost wages, the rescuers sobered up very quickly. It is reported that one of them said, "It would have been cheaper to fly in a veterinarian."

Red Dog's most reliable means of transportation was the Hamersley workers' bus that went between Karratha and Dampier on a regular schedule. Red Dog always chose his own seating arrangements. In trucks and cars, he rode only up front next to the driver. On buses, he always took the seat just behind the driver. His stubborness was exhibited by his insistence on these seating arrangements. New employees had to be educated. One new employee, a young woman, was initiated by Red Dog when she did not understand why he needed to occupy the entire seat. Therefore, day after day, she tried to push him over toward the window. Red Dog edged her off his seat daily for almost two weeks. Finally, without any observable reason, he allowed her to share his seat on a regular basis.

One day, Nancy Gillespie found Red Dog at her back door. She let him in only to find him covered with ticks.

As she begun to remove the ticks, she found two bullet holes in one of his ears. She took him to the local veterinarian, Rick Finney, who treated him over the next few years. When Dr. Finney first started his practice, he said he was baffled by the dog's seemingly endless supply of owners. On almost every visit, Red was accompanied by someone new. This, of course, was testimony to Red Dog's endless network of caring friends. Always cooperative when he was poked and pricked, he learned to visit the veterinarian on his own when a medical problem arose. Red Dog just seemed to know the right place to go for a particular problem. He knew where to find air conditioning in the summer. He knew where to find hamburgers and he knew that there were tasty barbequed steaks on the Dampier beaches.

The Gillespie family lived in a trailer park, run by the Hamersley Company. Red Dog frequently spent time with them. However, dogs were not supposed to live in the park, although several people owned pets. Park residents simply hid their animals when word went out that the caretaker was coming. But the caretaker spotted Nancy with Red Dog on several occasions and warned her that they would be evicted from the park if she kept him. Ignoring the edict, Nancy allowed Red Dog to stay with them whenever he chose to do so. Unfortunately, one morning the caretaker's wife spotted Nancy with Red Dog. After a nasty argument, the caretaker sternly informed the Gillespies that their trailer would be towed out of the park the following morning.

The next morning, park residents parked their cars, bumper to bumper, around the entire block, effectively obstructing the plan to remove the Gillespies. The sight of the cars so enraged the caretaker that he threatened to kill Red Dog. This threat was the last straw for Nancy

Gillespie who immediately drove over to the Hamersley Office in Karratha and told her story. That afternoon, a delegation of Hamersley workers paid a visit to the caretaker and his wife. The following day, the caretaker's family was gone and the park manager was looking for a new caretaker.

As time went on, Red Dog seemed to age prematurely. He became easily exhausted, had a cough, and lost considerable weight. When Dr. Finney examined him, he found that Red had heartworm disease. This disease is very serious and requires six weeks of daily treatments. How could Red Dog be kept in one place for six weeks? An answer came when members of the Roebourne Council were persuaded that this dog belonged to the people, not any one person. Therefore, they arranged for the dogcatcher to be responsible for the treatments at the dog pound. Red Dog was then placed in the pound where he received his daily medication.

Bewildered by his confinement, he nonetheless was very cooperative. Red Dog assumed the role of head pound dog, never mingling with those who had been arrested. One night, however, someone not understanding the situation let all the dogs out of the pound, apparently in an effort to release Red. It all worked out, however. Red found the dogcatcher and went back to the pound willingly to finish his treatments.

Red Dog lived a while longer, roaming his familiar places and always finding food, shelter, and friends. Then one day, Red Dog apparently found or was given some poisonous bait, probably strychnine. He began to have convulsions, became uncoordinated, and showed signs of brain damage. Reluctantly but mercifully, his friend and veterinarian, Rick Finney, put him to sleep. Dr. Finney kept Red Dog's collar and tag. One side of his tag says, "Red Dog - Bluey." On the other side, it reads, "I've been everywhere mate."

The next day Australian newspaper headlines announced Red Dog's death on November 21, 1979. The Hamersley Iron News described him as "The Pilbara's Own Epitome of the Dog Liberation Movement." Another headline read, "Red Dog, 1971-1979. Died by the Hand of Man."

Almost immediately a committee was set up to raise money to pay Dr. Finney. He refused any payment so the first money raised was used to start a memorial to this brave and courageous dog. Radio and newspapers brought in more money. Tourists from the entire continent responded. People not only gave money for the memorial, but many were so moved that they wrote poems about the dog. Red was buried outside of Roebourne. His memorial statue sits on a 10-ton iron ore rock which came from the Mt. Tom Price mine. It is located in the Information Bay at Dampier, Australia, only about a hundred yards up the road from where his friend, John Stazzonelli, was killed on his motorcycle. All their friends hope that they have been reunited.

The statue was created by Mrs. Merri Forrest of Perth. She donated her services saying, "I was happy to sculpt Red Dog as a tribute not only to him, but to all dogs who have made life happier for people in pioneering Australia." The monument reads, "RED DOG, the Pilbara Wanderer, died November 21, 1979. Erected by the many friends made during his travels."

Greyfriars Bobby of Edinburgh

The Story of a Dog's Loyalty

Just south of Edinburgh, a litter of Skye terriers was born in 1858. One they called Bobby, named after Bobby Burns. This area of Scotland breeds the smallest and shaggiest of all the Skyes. "You can scarcely see the dog for the coat," is a common remark about these dogs which used to be the favored pet of nobility because of their alertness, elegance, dignity, and cheerfulness. The Skye terrier is also fearless and loyal, the two characteristics that dominate the story of Bobby.

Bobby's thick thatch of silver gray hair protected him from the harsh winters of northern Scotland. Bobby's body grew only to a little less than two feet long, supported by six inch legs. Growing up, he was pursued, much to his displeasure, by his owner's young daughter who liked to pick him up and hug him. Bobby much preferred to spend his time with Auld Jock, the hired hand, a shepherd who tended the sheep, the cattle, and the crops. Bobby loved Auld Jock better then anyone he knew.

Bobby particularly looked forward to going to the city on the hay wagon with Auld Jock. Every Wednesday Auld Jock drove to the Grassmarket area of Edinburgh's Old Town for the family's weekly supplies. When the daily time-gun (a cannon sitting on a high parapet of Edinburgh Castle) cracked through the air of the city at precisely one o'clock, Auld Jock and Bobby made it a custom to go to Ye Olde Greyfriars Dining Rooms owned by Mr. Traill. Mr. Traill was an educated merchant who could converse comfortably with all of his customers, regardless of their station in life. Both Auld Jock and Bobby would be served a warm, nourishing meal at his establishment. The old man and Skye puppy always sat in the same place, a far corner beside the fireplace at a window overlooking Greyfriars kirkyard. This church yard had an immense old cemetery dating back to the 17th century. Its many ornate tombstones, statues, time-worn monuments, and eroded tablets were crowded inside a stone wall. Auld Jock would look out the window for as much as a half hour. Sometimes he even seemed to look at the cemetery yearningly.

Before setting out for home after lunch, Auld Jock and Bobby often took a walk past the kirkyard which lay below Castle Rock, surrounded by the backs of shops and high slum tenement buildings that had once been fine mansions. On another side of the cemetery was Heriot's Hospital which was not a hospital at all. It was a charity school for the care and education of "puir orphans and faderless boys."

At the kirkyard gate was a sign reading "NO DOGS ALLOWED." One day when Auld Jock and Bobby passed by, the gate stood open. Bobby peeked in and spotted a cat. He let out a loud yip and went after the cat, chasing him over headstones, around vaults of illustrious people, and ended up in the play yard at Heriot's Hospital where all the "faderless boys" joined in the chase. When the caretaker, Mr. Brown, heard the commotion, he came running from his house next to the cemetery. When he caught up to the group, he scolded Auld Jock in front of all the onlookers. Greatly embarrassed, Auld Jock turned to Bobby and spoke harshly to him. Auld Jock apologized humbly as Mr. Brown quickly ushered them out of the cemetery yard. Months later, it was clear that Bobby never forgot that day.

Late in the fall, the weekly trip to town for supplies was different. Instead of Auld Jock, the landlord of the farm drove the wagon. Auld Jock just rode along silently with Bobby at his side. When the time-gun went off, Bobby and Auld Jock went to Mr. Traill's dining rooms as usual.

During these trips to the city, Bobby had developed a fondness for the soldiers parading through the streets with their kilts, white spats and bagpipes. He often left Auld Jock to look on for a while. On this particular day, when Bobby heard the soldiers coming he watched them for almost an hour. As a result, he had to run fast to catch up with the wagon on its way home. The wagon was halfway to the farm when Bobby caught up with it. He jumped on and immediately noticed that Auld Jock was not on the wagon. Bewildered and alarmed, he sprang off the wagon and ran frantically back to Edinburgh's Old Town to find him.

Auld Jock was a frail old man who had worked hard all his life just for a bunk, his meals, and a few pennies. He had been little more than a tool to most of his employers. He had never owned anything, had no relatives, and had never married. Now that Jock had become Auld Jock, he was no longer useful enough to be kept on at the farm, so he had been taken to the city to get along on his own as well as he could.

Bobby ran from one familiar place to another. Finally, he started searching in places he had never seen. Late in the evening he came upon a hole that had once been a cock-fighting pit. In a dark corner lay Auld Jock

IT TAKES A DOG TO RAISE A VILLAGE

sleeping. Bobby barked and barked with joy. He kept running around Auld Jock who did not waken, even when one of the neighbors yelled out a window demanding quiet. Bobby realized his barking was doing no good, so he took a running jump onto Auld Jock's legs, dug his claws into his legs, pushed his wet muzzle into his face, and barked in his ear. Auld Jock shook himself awake and finally said, "Eh, Bobby, er ye pleased with yerself? Yer Jock is fair silly today," and gave Bobby a hug. Bobby's world was finally right again.

Soon it started to rain and it kept raining until the pit began to fill with water. Bobby literally barked Auld Jock out of the pit. Because Auld Jock staggered and kept stopping as he tried to walk, Bobby nipped and begged him to follow. Finally, Bobby got him to the Greyfriars Dining Rooms where he knew there would be food and warmth.

Because of the severity of the storm, Mr. Traill had no business when Auld Jock and Bobby came through the door. Mr. Traill saw immediately that the old man was gravely ill. He gave Jock some dry clothes and fed them both. Mr. Traill offered to get a doctor, but Auld Jock shouted an emphatic, "No." A doctor was a terrible threat to a poor man in those days. Mr. Traill's offer to take him to an infirmary was met with even greater vehemence.

As the evening wore on, Auld Jock's breathing became increasingly labored. Mr. Traill became so alarmed he decided to go fetch a doctor in spite of Auld Jock's protests and the bad weather. He was not gone long, but when he returned with the doctor, both Auld Jock and Bobby were gone. Mr. Traill's feeling of guilt about his action remained with him for the rest of his life. He had caused Auld Jock and Bobby to go back out into the storm all because he had insisted on fetching an expensive and much-feared doctor.

Auld Jock somehow managed to get to a slum where he knew a woman who rented rooms. He hid Bobby in the pocket of his great wool cape, knocked on the door, and paid the woman a week's rent. When he got to the room, Bobby jumped out of the cape pocket. To please Auld Jock, Bobby did all of his tricks—rolling over, jumping, turning on his back legs, and begging with a loud series of barks. The latter brought the landlady as well as other neighbors to their door. Auld Jock looked sternly at Bobby and said, "Hod yer gab or they'll put us oot." Bobby was crushed by this stern rebuke, but the agitated neighbors quieted down and Bobby never barked in that room again.

Throughout their first night in this cold, dreary room, Auld Jock slept restlessly as his fever continued to cloud his thinking. Bobby watched closely. Once Auld Jock woke for a short time. While he was awake, he counted the money in his bag. "There's enough," he said. Then he read his Bible briefly. As his eyes wearied, he put his money on the Bible and laid his head back on a pillow. His breathing stopped several hours later when he went into his final sleep. Bobby was both bewildered and saddened when his beloved Jock no longer talked to him.

Three days later, the landlady realized she had not seen Auld Jock since the night he arrived. She called the sheriff to enter the room. The sheriff was greatly moved when he learned that the man had no relatives. He was also stunned at the sight of the mourning dog and the contrast between the old man's obvious poverty and the amount of money on the Bible. The sheriff did his best to make appropriate arrangements.

They found Auld Jock's real name, John Gray, in the front of the Bible. Two policemen were called to carry Auld Jock's body downstairs where they laid him in a plain pine box. One of the policemen walked through the streets to round up six pallbearers who turned out to be an assortment of unclean and indifferent people who needed a shilling. As they carried Auld Jock to Greyfriars kirkyard, Bobby walked under the casket all the way. When they got to the gate, Bobby remembered not to bark or to chase anything.

He entered the cemetery with the group. After the casket was lowered into the ground, the gravedigger filled the hole, leaving a mound of fresh earth. He then urged Bobby to leave the kirkyard with him, but Bobby refused. James Brown, the kirkyard caretaker, also tried to get him to leave, but he again refused. Mr. Brown, while sympathetic to the little dog, did not want to lose his job. So he set Bobby outside the gate, which he latched.

Bobby started digging under the gate, but he could not make enough room underneath the gate to get through, even after his paws bled from his efforts. Giving up, he stayed quietly at the gate and waited. Later on in the evening, a woman drove up to the gate in a carriage. She stepped out of her carriage and opened the gate to let herself into the kirkyard. It was then that Bobby slipped in and lay down on Auld Jock's grave for the first time.

Five days later, just after the hour of one o'clock sounded, Bobby sneaked out of the cemetery to find Mr. Traill. Mr. Traill was shocked to see that Bobby was alone and nearly starved. After a dish of haggis and a nice sleep, Mr. Traill and Bobby left the dining rooms together. Mr. Traill was confident that the "wee dog" would lead him to Auld Jock. He followed him to the kirkyard gate where Bobby danced and begged to be let inside, but he did not bark. Seeing the urgency in the dog's eyes, Mr. Traill opened the gate, and Bobby led him straight to a new unmarked grave. Suddenly, Bobby heard Mr. Brown enter the cemetery yard and quickly disappeared. The two men engaged in conversation. Mr. Traill told Mr. Brown the story of his going for a doctor. It was then that Mr. Brown came to realize that it was Auld Jock and Bobby he had thrown out of the cemetery the previous month.

The two men started searching for Bobby. Some of the slum children had heard the story and came to help in the search for the "puir wee dog." Not finding him, the children finally went home and the two men sat on a tipped slab memorializing a "Mistress Jean Grant" to discuss the situation. Mr. Traill decided to notify the rightful owner of the dog the following week; until then, Bobby could stay at the dining rooms if they could find him.

They started whistling and calling him. In just a few moments, Bobby came out from under Mistress Grant's tombstone right where they were sitting! Bobby followed Mr. Traill to his dining rooms for dinner, but ran to the door to be let out as soon as he had finished eating. Mr. Traill refused to let him out. Bobby decided to earn his way by doing Mr. Traill the favor of killing a rat that was in the corner of the dining rooms. But Mr. Traill still refused to let him out. Bobby then began to bark until he created such a disturbance in the dining rooms, that he finally got his way.

When Mr. Trail opened the door to let Bobby out, two slum boys, Geordie Ross and the lame Tammy Barr, on crutches, were outside playing in the street. Mr. Traill asked them if they would sneak Bobby into the kirkyard for a shilling. They were delighted to be part of such intrigue and they really wanted to help this loyal little dog. They also knew an inconspicuous way of entering the cemetery, and they certainly could use the money.

The following Wednesday, Bobby's rightful owner, having received the message, went to Mr. Traill's dining rooms and got Bobby. The farmer put Bobby in a basket, strapped the lid down, and put the basket in the wagon. As they rode along, Bobby pushed his nose out a hole in the basket so that he could capture all the smells that would help him to return where he belonged once he freed himself. When they arrived at the farm, the little girl was ecstatic to see Bobby, but she was told he could not go in the house with her. He had to be kept in a fenced yard for the night so he would not run away again.

The minute Bobby was alone, he started digging and

digging under the fence. Fatigue and sore paws did not stop him. Skye terriers are known for their persistence regardless of the odds. Exhausted and aching, he finally squeezed through a little hole and started running back to Greyfriars kirkyard. It was difficult because Bobby often found himself in places he had never been, but at last he reached a hill where the smells of Edinburgh reached him. He slipped into the kirkyard just before Mr. Brown latched the gate for the night. When Bobby lay down on Auld Jock's grave this time, it began to snow. It was the beginning of winter.

Bobby became tired of hiding from Mr. Brown under Mistress Grant's slab, so he started to kill rats and mice, collecting them in a far corner of the yard. One morning he ran straight up to Mr. Brown and showed him his collection. Mr. Brown was overwhelmed, "Guid work, a brae dog, and an uncanny fetcher." Mr. Brown decided Bobby should meet Jeanie, his wife. From that day forward, Bobby took supper with the Browns and spent his nights on Auld Jock's grave. He no longer had to hide.

As winter invaded Scotland, the cemetery was usually deserted. However, some of the slum children (Ailie Lindsay, Tammy Barr, Sandy McGregor, and Geordie Ross) would slip into the kirkyard and play with Bobby almost every day. Bobby allowed no one but the children to hug and scratch him. He grudgingly let Jeanie Brown give him baths. This little dog had found a lot of good friends who would take care of him.

Eventually, the Greyfriars church minister, Reverend Lee, was told of the dog's living arrangements. Bobby was not quite as big a secret as Mr. Brown had thought. Reverend Lee had met Bobby quite by accident one evening and wondered when he would learn about him officially. Reverend Lee was equally sympathetic to the situation, so he spoke to the elders individually, apparently adding them to the growing number of supportive conspirators.

As the years went by, Bobby endeared himself to two generations of slum children and Heriot school lads. He spent his days guarding the nests of wrens, robin redbreasts, and skylarks. Indeed, the birds often fearlessly landed on Bobby's back. They trusted him because he drove off their predators—cats, mice, and rats.

Bobby had a routine. He had lunch with Mr. Traill, played in the afternoons with the children, took dinner with the Browns and spent his nights on Auld Jock's grave regardless of the weather. The children called him a "bonny doggie" and a "sonsie (warm hearted) tyke."

When Bobby was about eight years old, two disturbing events happened at Mr. Traill's dining rooms on the same day. The little dog had become very well known for his one o'clock visits to the dining room corner where he and Auld Jock had once had lunch. One day Sergeant Scott, a soldier in the Queen's army living in the castle, asked to buy the dog. When Mr. Traill said Bobby was not his to sell, the soldier said, "Some day I will kidnap him so he can cheer all the lonely men in the castle." The soldiers loved dogs and even had a canine cemetery on the castle grounds.

The same day, a policeman came in for lunch and commented that Bobby did not have a license. Mr. Traill had an ominous feeling about these events as he locked up his dining rooms that night.

A week later, Mr. Traill and Bobby received a summons to appear in court. The magistrate in charge was stern, stating that the dog would be destroyed if Mr. Traill did not get him a license which would cost seven shillings. Mr. Traill said that the person named on a license had to take responsibility for the animal, and he could not be responsible for a dog he saw only one hour a day. This situation reinforced the concern Mr. Traill had about Bobby's fate if something happened to either Mr. Brown or himself. The magistrate was very impatient and about to dispose of the case when a messenger entered the room and handed him a note. After reading it, the magistrate seemed to change his demeanor. He suddenly moved the case to the St. Giles police office for the following week.

The slum children had heard this news and became concerned, especially about the money. They did not realize that Mr. Traill could not only afford the seven shillings, but he would never let Bobby die. However, the children were terrified. They would do anything to see that Bobby would not be put to death for want of seven shillings—which was a fortune to them.

They took action. Ailie and Tammy ran through the slums in desperation. Some children gave their milk money. Everyone who knew Bobby sacrificed something. When Ailie and Tammy finished canvassing the slums, they had only five shillings. In tears, Ailie ran to the dormitory where the University students lived, asking, "Do ye new the wee Bobby?" Fortunately, she ran into Geordie Ross, a Heriot lad who was studying to be a physician. He said, "Losh! I wish I had as many shullings as I had guid times with wee Bobby and paid naething." Geordie gave them two more shillings, and they ran to St. Giles where Bobby's case was being heard.

The prestigious Lord Provost of Edinburgh's courts now had the case. When the story of Bobby was told to him once again, he smiled and told Mr. Traill that the case had been taken care of. All of this took place not in a court of law but in St. Giles cathedral. While the Lord

Provost and Mr. Traill were still talking, the children found them. They came running in, dropping the pennies and half pennies on the altar, hoping they were not too late. When they looked around and saw Bobby, they yelled, "Bobby's no deid!"

Tammy, with his crutches, and all the other children in their tattered clothing ran to play with Bobby. The Lord Provost did not dare refuse the outpouring of so much love. Later, he would find another good cause where their money could be used. The Lord Provost lifted Bobby high up in the air. He also held up a fine leather collar which he passed to the children so that each one could get a close look. The shiney brass plate attached to the collar read, "GREYFRIARS BOBBY from the Lord Provost 1867 Licensed." The Lord Provost's eyes were misty as he watched firsthand the love and affection this dog had engendered in these unwashed, poverty-stricken children dressed in rags. The children were unaware of all this. They were preoccupied with expressing the tender affection they felt for this little dog who had brought so much to their drab lives.

The Provost spoke to the children about caring for Bobby, now and when he died. Because when Bobby died, he said, he would not be allowed to be buried in the cemetery so the children would need to make appropriate arrangements for him. The children listened to every word. Then the Lord Provost put the collar on Bobby and held him up in the air to show how grand he looked. Finally, Tammy broke the silence and said, "We'll gie 'im a grand buryin'. We'll find a spot beneath a hawthorne whar the blackbird whustles." Then they all left St. Giles together. The children understood their responsibility and their eyes shone with pride for having been given this opportunity.

Not long after these events, Bobby spent part of an afternoon at a soldier's parade, bagpipes and all. As he walked along watching the tassles on the spats, the soldier who had threatened to kidnap Bobby did just that. He grabbed Bobby up in his arms and carried him to the castle where all the soldiers enjoyed watching Bobby do all the tricks Auld Jock had taught him. As dusk came, Bobby began to run around wildly. He could not find a way out. The dog-lover among the soldiers wanted to show off Bobby's beautiful eyes. He lifted him up on his lap. First, he found the Lord Provost's collar which he decided was some kind of a canine Victoria Cross. Then, when he pulled the veil of hair back from Bobby's eyes, he was shocked at the grief he saw. The soldier yelled, "Get him back to the cemetery!"

But because of the thick fog, the soldiers decided to take Bobby back the next morning. However, as the night wore on, Bobby became more and more agitated. Finally, he jumped over a wall that led to a precipice going to the sea. Somehow, Bobby kept finding safer and more familiar ground. It took him hours. His feet bled. After his last jump, his back legs went numb so he had to drag himself painfully along to his destination.

Mr. Brown, Mr. Traill, and the children knew that something had happened to Bobby when he did not appear for supper. They spent the better part of the same evening looking for Bobby but, when the fog became too thick, they gave up. However, hoping that he might find his way, Mr. Brown left the kirkyard gate ajar—just in case.

The next morning, Tammy found Bobby half-alive on Auld Jock's grave. His screams brought Mr. Brown, his wife, and the other children. One of the children ran for Geordie Ross, the "Heriot lad" who was now a medical student. Geordie examined him all over, but found only severe bruises and sprains. He prescribed some medicine for pain, and suggested that the children take turns watching over Bobby for a day or so. Mrs. Brown brought him food and water. He was soon restored.

From that day forward, the children started a new ritual that lasted for the rest of Bobby's life. At nightfall, before the drum and bugle sounded from the castle, every child in the tenements opened a window and called out, "A guid nicht to ye, Bobby." In the morning, one by one, they called out, "A guid day to ye, Bobby." Because Auld Jock had forbidden him to speak in the kirkyard, Bobby would only answer by wagging his tail.

During the next five years, Bobby's celebrity status grew. He spent more and more time on Auld Jock's grave which was marked only by Bobby's presence.

People would pass by, shake his paw and often leave bits of food. One day, the Baroness Burdett-Coutts, a grand lady who loved animals, came all the way from London especially to meet Bobby. When she entered the kirkyard, Bobby sensed her warmth, so he trotted her straight to Auld Jock's grave. While the Baroness was standing at the grave, Ailie, who was now a well-mannered and trained housemaid, came by to see Bobby. She told the Baroness about growing up with Bobby and the pledge the children had taken that day five years ago. The Baroness looked deep into Bobby's eyes and saw the lingering grief that was becoming more and more unbearable. She told Tammy, "Be with him all you can, for I think his beautiful life is near its end. And please don't let him die before I return from London."

When the grand lady returned to Edinburgh a few weeks later, the Lord Provost who had recently been knighted by the Queen, was with her. Together, they spoke to the Greyfriars minister and elders about having Bobby buried with his beloved master, Auld Jock. It took a lot of talking, but it was finally agreed to, albeit reluctantly.

The Baroness had made another decision. She decided that there needed to be a monument of Bobby so that future generations would remember what love and devotion a small animal can bring to so many people. She believed that Greyfriars Bobby's life was a testimony to all the best in people and in animals. After much work, she was finally granted a place for the monument at the end of the George IV Bridge, opposite the main gateway to the Greyfriars kirkyard.

The Baroness then arranged for both a painter and a sculptor to spend many days with Bobby. A statue of Bobby sitting on top of a fountain and looking toward the kirkyard was planned. The Baroness returned on several occasions to see how the plans were progressing. The last time she returned to Greyfriars to check on the project, she laid a wreath of laurel on Auld Jock's grave. This may have been Auld Jock's only personal recognition. Bobby certainly appreciated the gesture. He gave her a warm thanks with a wagging tail and a warm lick of her hand.

When the Baroness departed, she said, "Goodbye, goodbye to you, the most loving and lovable wee dog in the world." Her tears fell on Bobby's curly coat and she departed. It has now been over a century that visitors from all over the world continue to visit the statue of Greyfriars Bobby, the "wee dog" whose story is a testimony of love, devotion, bravery, and loyalty.

Epilogue

Boozer, Patsy Ann, Lampo, Owney, Red Dog, and Greyfriars Bobby were basically strays—street dogs, so to speak. I prefer to call them community dogs because a community of people looked after them. They did not have easy lives, nor was it easy for the people who took responsibility for them.

Their friends clearly understood that the need for freedom dictated what the dogs wanted from them. The dogs always seemed able to find people who were willing to spend both time and money on them, but of course on their terms. There was, however, a continual problem with the laws. Leash laws and license laws were constantly violated.

There is another kind of ownerless dog; namely, the dog who is abandoned, mistreated, underfed, and unloved. Such animals are fortunate if they find their way to a humane society or a rescue group. Animal control agencies are obviously needed for these animals.

Somewhere between the extremes of a devoted owner and a negligent owner is the community dog, the one cherished by a town, a group of workers or a handful of citizens. These animal have no standing in the eyes of the law.

I have talked to several animal control officers who all say about the same thing. "If an animal does not have a license, we pick the animal up and put it out for adoption in five days. If the animal does have a tag, we call the owner. If the owner does not come in five days, the dog is put out for adoption." It is understandable that animal control officers must do this in the case of strays whose behavior is unknown or of any dog that may be a threat to the public. But if a dog's behavior is known to be safe and if its own welfare is not in jeopardy, it seems a pity that free-spirited dogs with loving and responsible human friends cannot find a legal niche.

It is this author's belief that pets humanize humans and that millions of us are better persons for having known and loved a pet. I am sure that the friends of the dogs in these stories would agree that their efforts on behalf of the dogs were well rewarded and that even if the dogs allowed it, it would have been cruel to try to constrain their way of life.